MW01516107

"A world without poetry
is beyond imagination"

~ Candice James

Other Books By Candice James

A Split in the Water *(Fiddlehead Poetry Books)* 1979
Inner Heart, a Journey *(Silver Bow Publishing*) 2010
Bridges and Clouds *(Silver Bow Publishing)* 2011
Midnight Embers *(Libros Libertad)* 2012
Shorelines *(Silver Bow Publishing*) 2013
Ekphrasticism *(Silver Bow Publishing)* 2013
Purple Haze *(Libros Libertad)* 2014
A Silence of Echoes *(Silver Bow Publishing)* 2014
Merging Dimensions *(Ekstasis Editions)* 2015
Colors of India *(Xpress Publications India)* 2015
Short Shots *(Silver Bow Publishing)* 2016
City of Dreams *(Silver Bow Publishing)* 2016
The Water Poems *(Ekstasis Editions)* 2017
The 13th Cusp *(Silver Bow Publishing)* 2018
Fhaze-ing *(Silver Bow Publishing)* 2018
Haiku Paintings *(Silver Bow Publishing)* 2019

Rithimus Aeternam

Candice James

Silver Bow
Publishing

Box 5 – 720 – 6th Street,
New Westminster, BC
V3C 3C5   CANADA

3

Title: Rithimus Aeternam
Author: Candice James
Copyright © 2019 Silver Bow Publishing
Cover Painting: "Ghost Trees of the Violet Waters" Candice James
Layout/Design: Candice James
ISBN: 9781774030585
ISBN: 9781774030592

Library and Archives Canada Cataloguing in Publication

Title: Rithimus aeternam / Candice James.
Names: James, Candice, 1948- author.
Description: Poems.
Identifiers: Canadiana (print) 20190201460 | Canadiana (ebook) 20190201509 | ISBN 9781774030585 (softcover) | ISBN 9781774030592 (HTML)
Classification: LCC PS8569.A429 R58 2019 | DDC C811/.54—dc23

Email: info@silverbowpublishing.com
Website: www.silverbowpublishing.com

Preface:

I was fortunate to have my first book of poetry A SPLIT IN THE WATER (100 pages) published in 1979 by Fiddlehead Poetry Books, University of New Brunswick. At the time, I didn't realize how lucky I was to have a book published by Fiddlehead and even more fortunate to have Fred Cogswell (editor of the Fiddlehead and officer of the Order of Canada) as my mentor. And because I didn't realize this, I didn't capitalize on the opportunities Fred offered me to publish more books of poetry by me. I was in the middle of switching horses in mid-stream so to speak and was firmly ensconcing myself in the music scene as a musician and singer-songwriter in a professional band.

Fred and I kept in touch and he kept asking me to send more poems, and I kept saying I would for sure when I got back home; but alas, I never did get around to it, although I did keep writing poetry throughout the years. Fred passed away in 2004 and that was the same year I hung up the band scene and in 2010 I came full circle back to poetry and was appointed Poet Laureate of the City of New Westminster, BC CANADA.

In the early years I started out writing free verse with a sparse sprinkling of rhyming poetry; and then in 2009 I decided to force myself to write ten Shakespearian sonnets to see if writing in poetic form may have an influence on my free verse when I finished. Needless to say I had a very hard time forcing myself into structured form and at first truly hated writing sonnets; and then, a funny thing happened. When I was halfway through, around sonnet seven, I found myself quite enjoying the meter, iambic pentameter and rhyme scheme. I then went back to free verse and found it flowed so much better so I decided to write more rhyming poetry but not necessarily sonnet structure and I must say writing rhyme has came easier to me over the years and now it is almost second nature to me. I have found the more you do something, the better you get at it… like the old adage says… "practice makes perfect".

I hope you will enjoy this book of rhyming poetry and I have taken the liberty of using one of my own favourite rhyming poems as an introduction to this my 15th book of poetry alive with meter and rhyme.

~ *Candice James,* Poet Laureate Emerita, New Westminster, BC CANADA

Introduction/Author's Note:

I find myself looking backward to my younger days more and more with each passing year. I also find myself wondering at the trials and tribulations of those whose lives have been touched by the ravages of Alzheimer's Disease and its effect on their loved ones and family. This poem is my take on what it must be like for the person actually in the throes of the disease.

Turned Inside Out

Wandering into Alzheimer's night
I'm fading from reality's light.

I've forgotten the words to your favourite song
and the lyrics to mine don't seem to belong.
I can't tell the difference between right and wrong
and the memories I cherished are now lost and gone.

I reach for my cane as my hands start to shake.
I can't recall when my bones didn't ache.
I look in the mirror and see a white streak
has replaced the black strands of my widow's peak.
Then my mind starts to wander. My eyes glaze over;
I'm a child again running through fields of clover.

Looking back there are things I barely remember,
and January's now just a prolonged December.

I've learned many things from my sojourn on earth.
There's two sides to everything; each of great worth.
A whisper's the other side of a shout,
and today is just yesterday turned inside out.

Rithimus Aeternam

Table of Contents

WHIMSY ... 169

Surreal

Alive in the Paint

From shadow to light, purple to white,
nestled in between death and life
I pick up my brush in the candle-glow
to paint an emotion I know will flow
with passion, lust, love and romance,
fabulous rhythm and eloquent dance,
where the blessed, frail and obscurely quaint
are part of the brilliance, alive in the paint.

Then I take a step back, and step out of the picture.
I analyze the paint and survey the mixture.

I put down my brush and cross the floor,
gaze into the mirror that hangs on the door.
I stare at my image in shock and surprise
at the secrets hiding behind my eyes.
I see evidence of old truths tossed away
where guilty pleasures held court and held sway,
dipping my world into ebony ink,
clouding my judgement 'til I couldn't think;
couldn't differentiate right from wrong,
a symphony from a rock'n'roll song.

So, I polished my breath until it came to rest
on the satin lapel of an artist's vest.

Stars twinkled above as darkness undressed.
I fell to my knees and humbly confessed.
The world began spinning a bright shade of white
as I moved from the shadow into the light,
delighting the eye in the sky I suppose
because it applauded in quiet repose.
Now, if I listen closely I can still hear the sound
of that one hand clapping...the other one bound;
then the sound slowly fades, becomes very faint;
but something still breathes...
                                        alive in the paint

15

I Succumb

I was never the intended
I intended to be
although abstruse intention
eventually found me.

And I am hard pressed to relax
in the warm embrace of the night;
to leave the cold hard day behind
and let my weary mind unwind.

My tongue grows thick. It's hard to speak
as sleep creeps in on small cat feet,
and beseeches me to succumb
to the numbness I've become.

And I am hard pressed to relax
in sleep's hammock peacefully;
although my eyes grow heavy
they refuse to close completely.

And I am hard pressed to relax
in the fallout of cruel surprises,
trying to elude my enemy
in war-torn and tattered disguises.

They can't save me from becoming the intended
I never intended to be;
and they can't stop abstruse intention
from eventually finding me.

And though I am hard pressed, I will continue on;
a marauder wandering through broken dreams and songs,
stumbling in the darkness further from the sun
until finally I succumb
to the numbness I've become.

Poets' Dance

Hazy circles of possibilities
vibrate and float haphazardly touching down,
onto the jagged squares of quiet desperation,
in deafening silence without a sound.

Inside this massive silence,
that holds all the answers ,
we remain the unanswered questions;
the pantomime dancers.

> *All things pass away; then come to pass again.*

Do not wait to step into the sunshine of your soul;
the best part of you is beckoning you to open the scroll
and step into the sacred circle of the poets' dance:
where quicksilver lightning blends dreams with romance
shaking the spirit's eternal foundations
and rocking the cradle of great expectations.

It keeps spinning toward you, that wheel of fate,
waiting for you to step up to the plate.
So, pick up the bat and hit that home run.
Lay claim to whatever dreams may come.

Follow the path of quills and ink stains
that never washes aways with the rains;
and engrave the surreal letters of life and breath
onto the well-worn parchment of death.

> *All things pass away; then come to pass again.*

We are all searching for the God particle,
quite unaware that we are the God particle.
The answers you seek are not found
somewhere out there in the vast expanse.
They're inside YOU! Look inward angel …
and step into the poets' dance!

17

Sonatastice Perpetuum

A ribbon of hard sound reverberates
in my reverie; it shakes and wakes
a parlour of numb nerves, a long time asleep,
into a brand-new world that can't weep.

I witness blue music climbing green mountains
to find a lost glade of pristine fountains.
Borne from the deepest scar on despair's face,
a raincloud scales a luminous staircase
that blinds the frail and frivolous eye
sewing it shut so it can't cry.

I'm reborn and baptized in sleek symphonies
of sweet sound and glorious mysteries,
filled with ear-piercing highs and heart wrenching lows.
It's all moving too fast and then it slows.
I lose control and my bearings once more
while searching for Nirvana's lost score
hiding behind a blue bubble door.

I wallow half frozen in quicksand's mire.
My matches are wet and I can't light a fire.
At the core of this tinder-box dry rot forest
dead birds are singing an out of tune chorus;
and the *Lord of the Flies* is the crazed composer
conducting this bizarre operatic exposure
played on a cracked didgeridoo,
turning you into me and me into you
in a scotch and soda watered down score;
and I just can't take this bliss anymore.

It's too beautiful to listen to and remain sane.
Borne of never-ending relentless rain
and divine despair's greatest living pain:
sonatastice perpetuum again and again,
now ad infinitum for the true insane.

Crumbling Prison

The skeletons I incarcerated so long ago,
in the cellular structures of my soul,
claw tooth and nail with long bony fingers,
at this moment of truth and a memory that lingers
in the crumbling prison locked in my mind
where time and tide start to unwind.
A ghost from the past whispers and calls
through gaps in these dark gray concrete walls.
I can hear the distant rattle and clunk
of petrified bones in a rusted-out trunk
growing much louder as they draw near
my large guarded castle, my fortress of fear;
the dark burned out building I keep my dreams in,
where there's nowhere to end, and no place to begin.

Each skeleton was part of a dream that died.
A wish that ran away but couldn't hide.
These long-time residents haunting my dreams
hide in the dark at the edge of my screams.
Though I fight, incessantly, to set them free,
they cling, like wool, to me steadfastly.
So, I draw out my pistol and ready my sword
to sever, at last, their umbilical cord
and force these skeletons to take their leave.
God is my witness. Their blood's on my sleeve.

These skeletons I incarcerated so long ago
in the cellular structures of my soul
have taken their leave like thieves in the night.
They've fashioned their bones into wings, taken flight
flying far, far away from the weak, frail and blind,
leaving me to atone for my sins all alone
in this crumbling prison locked in my mind.

Cold Crisp Morning

Walking the beach on a cold crisp morning
a damp sky above imposes a warning.
Storm clouds droop in pale shades of gray
as a wild wind threatens to blow them away.

There's a bittersweet taste in the mouth of my dreams;
a sugary acid that tears at their seams.
I can feel the chill of second-hand breath
in this winter air of impending death.

So I walk a bit faster, try to outrun the rain
even though each step is riddled with pain.
These old knees have walked too many roads
and my back is aching from too heavy loads.

I hear a gull's lamentable cry.
I see an eagle soaring on high.
As a beautiful feather falls from the sky
a pensive teardrop falls from my eye
for the sun-swept beaches of yesterday
and the glory days that have faded away.

I've been waiting and waiting for what dreams may come;
wishing on falling stars, coming undone.

And now too much time has come and gone.
These old eyes won't witness another dawn.
So, I throw off my coat on this cold crisp morning,
paying no attention to the sky's dark warning.

Time's caught me off-guard and handcuffed my wrists.
My body's dissolving in teardrops and mists.
Storm clouds rip open and drown the day
and the wild wind of death blows me away.

The wild wind of death … just blows me away.

Darkness Undressed

I want to

         bend it
         and shape it
         into pure energy
               ever-expanding.

I searched for it,

         yearned for it and found it,
         burned for it and bound it
         into eternal fire
               never-ending.

The elusive dream

         has come to rest;
         a tender caress
               aflame on my breast.

               Sins are confessed,
               blessed and unblessed;

and finally …

               the darkness
                   has undressed.

I Stand

Inside a pool of hot shiny embers,
I move through squares with circular centers.
My eyes are bound with barbed wire and ice.
My mind's held tight in a platinum vise.
Wounded by knives that don't leave a mark,
I travel through perilous light years of dark.

At the edge of a cut glass precipice
I stumble through fog-laden landscapes and mist.
With scarred feet I balance on diamond dust;
then crumble in flakes of flesh, blood and rust.
I spin a metaphor in my head
and step up to dance with ghosts of the dead.

> *I stand out of time, out of place, out of synch*
> *and then in a heartbeat as quick as a wink;*

I'm hanging between disasters and hope,
clinging to a threadbare rope,
trying to climb out of this cold damp mire   .
to bathe in the core of life's red hot fire.
As I fall headfirst into the flame,
I swear I hear someone calling my name.

Reborn in the shadow of the sun,
wrapped in a teardrop coming undone,
my eyes are unbound; I've regained my sight.
I move from the shadows into the light.
burning the hands of time down to the wire,
fanning the flames I'm alive in the fire.

> *I stand out of time, ablaze with desire*
> *and burn in the flames until…*
> *I am the fire.*

Again and Again

I'm the breath and death of all things;
a wounded bird with fractured wings,
waiting to be born again;
and reborn again and again.

I've lingered in tall grasses and cold snows,
been vanquished and lost in the fading echoes
of long since buried and silenced bagpipes,
in mist on the moors and fog on hillsides.

I've become the laughter of saviours and saints.
A child running wild with bright finger-paints,
naked and vulnerable adrift on a sigh.
I've parted dark thunderclouds high in the sky.
I've casually slept in an angel's breath
and been stalked by the nemesis of my own death.
Slipping and sliding down rivers of silk
I've danced to strange songs of a haunting ilk.

I've succumbed to lust with a fervent desire
and jumped headfirst into passion's fire
as if I were an intricate part
of the pulse and beat of my lover's heart
as it echoed softly against my chest
sanctifying the sins I confessed.

I've witnessed droplets of silver ink
falling into the red blood I drink,
spilled from a lost angel's trembling lips,
staining the white of my fingertips.
I bear my cross for the world to see.
I carry my sins and sorrows with me
and yet they remain silent, unclear
to eyes that won't see and ears that won't hear.
With the best of intentions I've tried to do right.
I've reclaimed my soul from the dark side of night
hoping to graduate into the light.

I've worshipped in churches with blood stained pews.
I've gazed through iron bars and I've paid my dues.
I've read from white scrolls turned ashen and black.
I've been shot in the chest and stabbed in the back.
In the crush of dark powdered inhibition,
my bones have been charred beyond recognition.

> *Again and again...*
> *I'm the preparation not the meal.*
> *Again and again...*
> *I am the dampness not the rain.*

I've flown wingless alone through layers of air
arriving here but believing I'm there.
I leave bits and pieces of flesh behind
as scar tissue to remember me by
so you'll never forget I passed this way,
though today and yesterday pass away.

I'm the breath and death of all life,
the residue of heartache's strife,
     waiting to be shaped
            again;

       and reshaped ...
         again and again.

Silent Songs and Rubber Bands

Within the glaring truth of blurred reality
penury and punishments pass by fleetingly;
and breath and death dance hand in hand
to silent songs and rubber bands.

Above the rolling thunderclouds where rainbows are conceived,
beneath a tattered sky I stood and suddenly believed
a billion less a billion stars leaves nothing, only mist;
and as I peered into the mist I saw in ghostly tryst:
Heaven's angels chanting songs of love and sanctity
leading broken spirit souls into eternity.

Embraced by loving arms,
* held in an angel's sway*
*   swiftly from life's raw nightmare*
*   I was swept away*

A sinner, now repented, I shed my soiled clothes,
and like a newborn phoenix, slowly I arose,
to dance to silent songs in resurrection's hall;
then suddenly without warning I heard a distant call.
A fluttering of angel's wings within a gathering throng
loosed the breath of heaven into a sacred song.

And then the sky ripped open,
with her golden gates flung wide,
and all God's chosen children were escorted inside

And I … I was amazed I was resting in God's palm,
safe forever from life's storms at peace within his calm

Inside heaven's domain I dance in mercy's glow
to silent songs and rubber bands and I have come to know
that breath and death walk hand in hand and are the kindred souls
beating God's eternal drum when the thunder rolls.

Fidelis Est Poetica

We're born to become never-ending breath
as we walk through the stages of life and death:
fidelis est poetica … the erudite soul.

In the cleansing fallout of a heavenly rain
there's an angel somewhere calling out my name
as they unwrap the seal and read from the scroll.

In spiritus perpetuum stars outrun the sun
as the tightly laced moon up above slowly comes undone
and dawn rubs the back of a weary midnight.

In spiritus perpetuum we transcend all time.
In rithimus aeternam we become the rhyme.
Faithful to poetry we walk in the light.

We are the breath of a God never-ending:
the diamond timepiece of the next dream pending;
the dreamer and all of the dreams that unfold.

We're born to become never-ending breath
as we walk through the stages of life and death:
fidelis est poetica … the erudite soul.

The Ashmodai Mirrors

(Ekphrastic poem written to Dina Goldstein's art photo of the same name)

In the dark of the black and the black of the dark,
captured inside a void cold and stark,
creating a flash fire from a dead spark,
an invulnerable ego in white left its mark.

The Ashmodai mirrors whispered and sighed
as the girl on the other side started to glide,
and into their universe she dimensionalized,
where there's nowhere to run and no place to hide.

She stood as a statue adorned with a smile,
stared into the mirrors and all the while
her alter egos looked on from behind
as a façade of sins began to unwind
on a spool of indifference, fragile and blind,
and a contract written in blood and designed
to capture her spirit and keep her confined
in a series of sentences coarse and unkind.

The room's atmosphere became heavy and cloyed.
The blood in her heart escaped into the void.
She fidgeted like a woman chased by her own ghost
hanging loose on the arm of an ungracious host
that still filled her body with passion and lust.
Her alter egos looked on in disgust
and watched as her soul turned from silver to rust
as she shrunk from herself and crumbled to dust.
They knew she'd destroyed their circle of trust,
So, they fashioned their bones into wings and took flight
flying far from the mirrors, the dark and the night.

She stepped back from the mirrors and with all her might
she opened her heart and moved into the light.
The Ashmodai mirrors whispered and cried
as the girl disappeared on the other side.

Play *'The Rose'* For Me

(Ekphrastic poem written to painting of the same name by Lavana La Brey)

She rises high above the music
in keys and esoteric tones,
drifting through Nirvana nights
and metaphysical zones.

Clad in velvet, satin and lace;
and shades of gray and black and white,
the piano keys become stepping stones
leading her softly into the light.

Old melodies cascade and flow
on a rolling scroll of hazy thought
and what this lady most would seem
that is what she most is not.

Wishing on a midnight star,
wrapped in a long ago memory,
she softly states her wistful plea;
she whispers … "Play *'The Rose'* for me."

Wisdom's Stone

So tired of hiding under wisdom's stone
I cast my fate onto a wild west wind.
Old hobos gathered round and set the tone,
reciting stories they could not rescind.
I spied from the left corner of my eye
a homeless beggar clothed in dreams of gold.
The dreamer of my dream was passing by;
he offered me a story I could hold.
My palm pulsated with the written word
and sparkling diamonds spilled from polished coal
In poetry and songs I'd never heard,
imploding rapture deep within my soul.

Adorned in ragged poetry and songs,
I write and sing to rid the world of wrongs.

A Wisp of Haze

I heard a weary voice inside my head;
a wisp of haze and then your body rose.
Magnificence shone on the ghostly dead.
You stood oblivious in silver clothes.

You did not notice me as I stood there.
I tried to grasp your hand, but it dissolved.
You sat down in your favourite easy chair;
a wisp of haze and then the room revolved.

Old memories flew round like mockingbirds
that brought with them a few unwelcome strays.
I saw you move your lips in silent words,
before you disappeared into the haze.

Tonight I'll wait for you to reappear
inside the hardened edges of a tear.

Somewhere Inside Eternity

The waxing indigo veil of night
shawls over Columbia Street
and somewhere inside eternity
the past and present meet.

A battalion of hazy engineers
digs into the heart of the city
to resurrect lost relics
buried in antiquity.

These ghostly archeologists
populate the dark of night
blending with the fog and mist
inside the fading light.

Now, in the year two thousand eighteen
the streets are packed with bikes and cars,
pedestrians, scooters and traffic lights
and neon signs that blot out the stars.

The days of simplicity are long gone,
and yesterday's safety nets torn and frayed.
We've lost the sweetness of the song
and the message it conveyed.

Somewhere inside eternity,
dissolving in the fading light,
yesterday and today pass by
like strangers in the night.

Shooting Stars

The colours collide, bump and grind
on the stark white canvas of my mind.
Trees emerge in kaleidoscope dance;
branches and leaves dip, sway and prance
in the arms of the wind's come-hither voice.

I hear a whispering melody
half-remembered and flowing free
in the misty canyons of yesterday
where ghosts of the past frolic and play
in the attic's playground of lost toys.

In the distance ebbing and flowing I see
a door at the edge of my memory
where stands the ghost of a younger me
chained to a wish I couldn't set free
trapped in the tumble of hours and years.

Inside this cage of ice-riddled time
I stand on a quarter and spin on a dime.
Deeds good and bad pass by on parade
and slowly this dream I call life starts to fade.
I bequeath to the world my treasury of tears.

Like shooting stars, we burn and crash;
here for a moment and gone in a flash.

Moonbeam and Twilight

There's a moonbeam on my shoulder,
a pale twilight chasing me down.
I wander a highway of burnt-out stars
dressed like an outlaw clown.

A haunting echo rings in my ears;
its sad overtones bring me to tears.
I walk down a trail of sharp broken glass.
I hear a voice whispering, "this too shall pass".

A stir of angels is writing new scripture
forging in fire a sacred signature
onto the touchstone of eternity
held in the waters of infinity.

My moment is passing without hesitation
and I've moved so far beyond expectation.
I'm merely a small blip on a large map;
a branch on the tree of life starting to snap.

I'm lost in a looping one-sided thought
tossed between freezing cold and icy hot.
The universe always sees through my disguise
my sighs, my lies and my alibis.
The last things I see as death closes my eyes:
the moonbeam and twilight twist in turn-about,
and the highway of stars is flickering out.

The Fevered Clutch of Eternity

On a misty, moonlit November night
I watch shadow people passing by.
I stand beneath a buttered streetlamp,
the atmosphere heavy and damp.

With fading breath and pale heartbeat,
the sleeping park across the street,
now silenced by an invading dark
still whispers secrets to the stars.

An ebony blanket covers the green.
A surreal hush envelops the scene
intermittently interrupted by
a scatter of raindrops from the sky.

I drift across a mirrored lake.
Tides wash over my virgin mindscape
and carve my signature in the shoreline.
I stand imprisoned inside its design.

I am a willing hologram
inside a feigned reality;
and believing this to be the truth
seems unseemly insanity.

But, there's a continuity
that runs the depth and breadth of me
turning rock solid dreams to streams
in the fevered clutch of eternity.

Beneath a hot buttered streetlamp
the atmosphere sultry and damp
I stand in spiritual bliss
at the edge of a star-spun kiss.

A Broken Wind Chime
(a villanelle)

A snow cast heart is frozen in time,
unrecognizable, beating no more,
hanging beside a broken wind chime.
It's a silent creature in pantomime,
with muted songs, no music, no score.
A snow cast heart is frozen in time
robbed of its rhythm, robbed of it's rhyme,
locked in a steel cage, no window, no door,
hanging beside a broken wind chime.
In a bed of dampened dreams and burnt lime,
a remnant of what it was before,
a snow cast heart is frozen in time.
Inside this prismatic paradigm,
rainbows and teardrops refract in its core,
hanging beside a broken wind chime.
Evidence of love's most grievous crime,
abandoned on a desolate shore,
a snow cast heart is frozen in time
hanging beside a broken wind chime.

Copper Canyon
(Ekphrastic villanelle to the painting of the same title)
*both painting and poem by Candice James

The sun on high continues to bake
desert trees chiseled in stone.
A copper canyon begins to awake.

In the aftermath of a gentle earthquake
and the architecture of nature's bone
the sun on high continues to bake.

Beauty's created for its own sake
safe in the palm of a hallowed zone.
A copper canyon begins to awake.

It's seen the world buckle and break
and heard the trees growl and moan.
The sun on high continues to bake.

On a gathering wind, trees tremble and shake.
Green dreams drip from eternity's cone.
A copper canyon begins to awake.

Echoes resound in a burning snowflake
and a surreal atmosphere sets the tone.
The sun on high continues to bake.
A copper canyon begins to awake.

Love

Ink Stain in the Rain

The cruel wind scrapes and rapes
the soft supple satin drapes
in the cave of evening shade.
Under gun metal sky,
cracked, splintered and dry,
we play our tragic masquerade.

On the mantle of doom
and foreboding gloom,
we reach for this feeling we're chasing.
We can't quite grasp enough of it,
just a quicksilver touch of it,
this dream Daughter Time is erasing.

Then I feel your heart slip,
so I tighten my grip
on the trembling lip of this storm.
Your body's a river,
a fast running shiver,
and I can't seem to keep myself warm.
Engulfed by the ocean
and fading emotion,
you let go of my hand.
Tide sweeps you away
but bids my heart stay;
nothing is as we planned.
Waves wash me ashore,
lips parched evermore
never to taste yours again.

Love letters and pain,
left out in the rain,
became a fading ink stain.
Now, days without sun,
the moon's come undone
        and I?
                I've become the rain.

Rebellion of My Middle Ages

Gazing back through yesterday's pages
to the rebellion of my middle ages,
I zipped myself up in a mirrored cocoon
in the shallows of a sun-stretched afternoon.
I saw slanted ghosts in a distorted maze
as I danced out loud in a surreal haze.

What was I doing way back then
before I began my affair with the pen?
I was running away from the ghosts of death
in the shortened gasp of a borrowed breath.

Running in circles hungry for love,
searching, searching below and above;
courting disasters and dancing with dangers,
playing with fire and sleeping with strangers;
a renegade hanging out with rednecks,
playing head games with music and sex.

Faces drift by unrecalled, undefined,
just hazy memories crossing my mind.
So, I focus through my Versace shades
scanning for lost fellow renegades;
lovable losers and rag-tag rebels,
faded Romeos and jaded Jezebels.

In the rebellion of my middle ages,
thumbing through these dog-eared pages,
I see my life passing by in stages
as I slowly dissolve... into the pages.

Beyond the Shadow of the Veil

Beyond the shadow of the veil
of themes and dreams and schemes,
we walked our roads with grace and ease,
and danced on starlit seas;
and it was done, and we were one
and we will always be,
hand in hand beneath the sun,
together flowing free.

Present, future falling fast,
into living moments past,
we'll live inside each other's breath
where there's no never-ending death;
where all roads lead to love,
by grace of God above.
Where your road leads to me,
and mine to you shall be
tiled in marble ever after,
silver smiles and golden laughter;
and hand in hand we will climb
to the pristine edge of time
safe within each other's hold
where dreams cannot be bought or sold.

Yes, we will love each other more.
'Twill be again as 'twas before;
my heart handcuffed by your kiss,
your heart shackled to my wrist.
No separation will exist.
Love so strong it cannot twist,
but strong enough to bend.
My lover and my friend:
from time's inception to the end,
beyond the shadow of the veil.

East of Eden, West of Love

The bittersweet taste of summer wine.
Passion polishing love to a shine.
Reaching Nirvana then past the brink.
Watching it fade like invisible ink.

Promises crept away on scarred feet
stumbling down a dark dusty street.
Crippled by vows we didn't keep,
love bowed her head and fell asleep.

We limped away with wounded hearts,
victims of our own false starts.
We let the lies we kept within
chafe at our hearts and wear them thin.

Beneath a burnished sky of stars
we hid inside our wounds and scars.
Locked in the shadow of a doubt,
we watched the flame grow dim, burn out.

Passion stripped off her mask and disguise
revealing alibis, secrets and lies.
Love on the rocks. Paradise lost.
Words turned to dust; music to frost.

Teardrops scarred a scarlet moon.
Eclipse of the heart. Midnight at noon.
A silent song, a wordless rhyme;
two poets dancing out of time.

An angel sighed. Stars fell from above,
somewhere east of Eden, west of Love.

The Taste

Your heart was too brutal for loving.
Your teachers were too drunk with wine.
They could not lead you to wisdom.
They just left you standing in line.
Your jazz riddled song was abandoned
long before it began.
The original score was rebranded
and sold to an amateur band.

You never knew the taste of my hunger
or hungered for my taste.
Your heart was too brutal for loving
and oh... what a terrible waste.

You washed over me in passionate waves
in the dark of a night black as coal
grinding grace into fury
on the petrified stone of your soul.
Strangers in all ways but one,
in the height of passion's desire
undressed and coming undone,
you touched me with second-hand fire;
but still, even knowing this to be true,
I languished in the left-over embers
of something not quite resembling love
at the bittersweet edge of surrenders.

I fell through your loosened embrace
like dust from fallen stars;
and finally I walked away
with only my wounds and scars.

You never knew the taste of my hunger
Or hungered for my taste.
Your heart was too brutal for loving
And oh... what a terrible waste.
Oh, what a terrible waste!

Shadow Dancers

We shared precious slices of time,
cold drinks, hot jazz and poetic rhyme
locked in a burning question
searching for the elusive answer
indelibly marked and branded
each other's shadow dancer.

On a slice of time we danced into the lights;
Nirvana nights, and gossamer flights
wrapped in the warp of a Rorschach ink stain
to the edge of a dream and back again.

> In the shadow dance
> of our brief romance
> our slices of time
> began to unwind.

In seductive pantomime
and a haze of whiskey and wine
our brief romance ran out of time
flickered out and then flat-lined.

> Like fine champagne
> left out in the rain
> the bubbles burst
> and the kick disbursed.

Now...
ensconced in eternity's flame,
helpless pawns in destiny's game,
on the wheel of karma we rock'n'roll
burnt into the edge of each other's soul,
eternally marked and branded
each other's shadow dancer.

This Eve

What shall we do this evening dear?
What shall we do this eve?
Shall we stand, worlds apart together,
beside love's tomb to grieve?

Shall we shed a tear or two
or tell a tender lie?
Shall we stare at separate moons
or speak of days gone by?

Gone are the stained-glass hours
we rode through yesterday,
astride the champing hearts
of lovers in love's play.

Gone are the star-spun nights
that lit our eager hearts,
bleeding with lust and love
tangled in body parts.

The road that leads to yesterday
is overgrown and dense;
a vast perfidious shadow land
past all points of pretense.

And if we dared to speak the truth
we'd be forced to confess
the waning of the wandering years
has caused our hearts recess.

What shall we do this evening dear?
What shall we do this eve?
Let us stand, worlds apart together,
beside love's tomb … and grieve.

Ship of Dreams

My ship of dreams has tattered seams
and rigging torn and frail;
a broken mast of memory's past
shoring up its sail.

And all the live long while
no measure of a smile;
no consolation gleaned from happenstance;
a brief romance, a passing dance,
in cold fell clutch of circumstance.

All the days, a drifting haze.
The dimming of lights. Nondescript nights.
Years pass like fog, wet, waterlogged.

Then, later on some golden pond
your pale ghost may arise
to shine your smile into my eyes
and take my heart beyond
the earthly confines of this life
away from heartache's pain and strife;
where we can drift on ship of dreams,
seaworthy with tight seams;
a mast of sturdy elm
with two hearts at the helm,
and love that cannot fail
shoring up its everlasting sail.

I wait here in my ship of dreams
tattered at the seams
wishing on a distant star
and wondering where you are ...
wondering where you are.

The Blue of a Fading Song

Trapped in the blue of a fading song
another long night lingers on;
the music and the dancers gone.

I'm lost on a street of shattered dreams,
unravelling night at its tattered seams,
searching for an ember or spark
to light my way out of this dark.

Trapped in the blue of a fading song
with notes and chords that don't belong
I stand at the edge of this broken night,
bathed in mystery and moonlight,
searching for you and yesterday
and distant dreams so far away.

Another long night lingers on;
the music and the dancers gone.
They've disappeared into the dawn;

but I remain …
trapped in the blue of a fading song.

Walking Through Mirrors

Walking through mirrors and surreal desire
I approach you tonight with decadent fire.
The stars begin turning the night inside out
destroying all fears and shadows of doubt.

I lie tangled up in your passionate kiss
stranded between a dream and a wish.
Too many nights I've died in your eyes
then been reborn in the depth of your sighs.

So, I'll lie in your heart like a wishing stone
carving my passion deep into your bone;
and to live in your eyes, your flame and your fire,
I'll keep walking through mirrors and surreal desire.

Soft on My Heart

July, the asphalt skillet sizzles,
melting away the day
as we travel toward the ocean.
A sun broiled city fades away.
as we slip through summer's loose embrace.

Your teardrops fall soft on my heart

We're caught in this belated spring
still trapped inside winter's sting
dangling on a quantum string
under a sparkling sky of bling.
No jewels of worth to be found here.
The sun about to disappear.

Your teardrops fall soft on my heart

The heat and passion burnt away;
buried in our yesterday.
Twilight shadows now unravel
looming on this road we travel.
I softly tighten my embrace
to ease the sorrow on your face;
and as we go our separate ways
fading music bends and sways.

Your teardrops fall soft on my heart;
       so soft on my heart,
            indelibly staining my soul.

Whispering Through the Blue

(Tribute for Rex Howard 1930-2012 British Columbia Country Music Hall of Fame Inductee 2004)

In serenades and ballads
your memory lingers on,
whispering through the blue
of a fading song.

If I listen, I can hear you
singing soft and low,
star-dusted melodies
in twilight's afterglow.

The sweet of the steel;
guitar riffs and strums;
the groove of the bass;
the beat of the drums.

The sweet, salty, powdered,
sugar dreams of yesterday,
tug gently at my heart strings
and then I drift away.

If I close my eyes
I can still hear you play
those old favorite songs,
that familiar swing and sway.

The sparkle and shine
of your music's refrain;
I hear your voice echoing
in shadows of the rain.

In serenades and ballads
your memory lingers on,
whispering through the blue
of a fading song.

Crayons to Perfume

I've been loving you from crayons to perfume.
Since I learned to tie my shoes, I've always followed you.
When you smiled at me, right then and there I knew
I'd be loving you from crayons to perfume.

When we were little kids, I held your hand watching cartoons.
Since those days of innocence, we've travelled many moons:
From strolling down a country road to walking down the aisle;
two-stepping through heaven I've cherished every mile.

We faced some hard times took the blows and still we carry on.
In moments of uncertainty your love keeps me strong.
Somehow you turn each heartache into a tender song
and I'll still be loving you when this whole world is gone.

I noticed the other day your hair is growing gray,
but in our hearts, we're still those kids at play just yesterday.
As your gray hair turns to white, I'll tighten my embrace
and trace the lines of love on your beautiful face.

Yes, I've been loving you from crayons to perfume
and when I can't tie my shoes, I'll still follow you.
When the crayons crumble and the perfume fades away
I'll still be loving you every step all the way …
from crayons past perfume.

Guitar Breeze

A lonely guitar breeze

                     strums
           the memories of his mind

           and everywhere he looks
               he finds

           short flashes of white,
             a fading twilight;

but no respite,
        no saving grace
               to light the night.

He's an outlaw riding
with an old dusty heartache
       and
  the dull fading glint
of an old rusty keepsake.

               There's emptiness
             all around
          in the cradle of night;

     And
with the dying of the light

               A lonely guitar breeze
              is stirring old memories
               never forsaken …

                 and some better left
                un-awakened.

Comes a Poet Darkly

In my midnight reverie comes a poet, darkly,
to room with candlelight decorated starkly.

His muscled body swiftly slides beneath a satin sheet
to feed a starving hungry heart wallowing in heat.
Limbs entwine and caution to the wanton wind is tossed.
Hearts re-sign, in blood red ink, love letters never lost.
Peeking through half-mast twilight the moon begins to rise,
flash dancing to love's amnesty shining in their eyes.
They ride the velvet tip of a double bladed sword,
these lovers that bought this feeling neither could afford.
Glistening with sweat, and spent, the lovers fall asleep
in supernatural mists that rock them in love's deep.
The moon winks out behind a cloud in dark skies overcast.
The lovers' ghosts then vaporize into memory's past
into the poem they once were centuries ago,
when rivers, valleys, mountains, were only amber glow.

The candle dims, the room swims with fading shadows starkly.
In my midnight reverie leaves a poet darkly.

The Deep Passionate Kiss

He's the promise of the rainbow after the rain,
the tender caress that soothes all my pain;
the whisper on my lips
when my composure slips.

He makes making love
always feel brand new:
a portrait in soft blue,
a panoramic view.

He leads me through
a wonderland of love:
the wind beneath my wings,
an angel from above.
He's all the joy life brings.

He's love in all its glory;
the start and end of my life story.

He's moonglow and mist,
the deep passionate kiss;
but much more than this,
he's the reason I exist.

On a Star Dusted Sea

On a star dusted sea
of midnight constellations
I dipped my pen
into the swirling aberrations,
creating a hand crafted epitaph
for the lovers who strayed from love's path
and walked out from the warm
into winter's storm.

Their tightly clasped hands
fell to their sides,
throwing caution to the wind
and the tides,
no longer to share familiar embraces,
turning the handle
to new feelings, strange faces.

Invisible now to each other,
faint ghostly apparitions
recalling slight perditions
yet making no admissions.

Were they ever really one
walking through sea and sun?
Or were they just a moment's bliss
forgotten like a summer's kiss?

Chilled by winter's icy bite,
sailing blind into twilight
with angels lost in flight,
I dip my pen once more
into the swirling night,
adrift on a star dusted sea,
alone, my lost angels and me.

I Close My Eyes

In the Mexican restaurant
wrapped in a mariachi beat I close my eyes
and for a fleeting moment
I'm in Mexico before I realize…

                                    I'm not.

Riding the skytrain at night
through transit zones and my own twilight zone
I close my eyes and feel you beside me;
your breath on my neck. I'm no longer alone…

                                          but I am.

Some days I prepare dinner
absentmindedly for two; not for one; not for four
subconsciously thinking I'll hear your voice
and you'll walk in, once again, through the door…

                                      but you don't.

There are nights; long, long and lonely nights
when I swear you are still here beside me.
I close my eyes
and for a fleeting moment you are here beside me…

                                      but you're not.

                    You are here with me
                    when I close my eyes;

                                so…
                                      I close my eyes.

Broken

In my dream last night, I withered and died.
In a split second, you were at my side
in this state of trance, this semi-death
in another dimension a brand new breath.

There are parallel worlds and strange universes
where dreams come true and overcome curses.
We were back together, our love new again,
bright, pure and pristine without a stain.

The light in the room was dim yet glowing.
We came to each other assured and knowing.
When we embraced we moved through each other
both well aware there could not be another.

Over many lifetimes we've climbed through our love.
As it is written below and above
together our journeys and lessons unwind.
We're tied by Akashic records that bind.

But alas the dawn unmasked the dream
And this fantasy world came apart at the seam.

In my dream last night, no words were spoken.
In my dream last night, we were not broken.

She Believes

She believes in heroes and knights in shining armour.
Romantic love stories and fairy tales still charm her.
She lives both in the public eye and in her private world.
She's a corporate woman but she's still a little girl.

She wakes up every morning and jumps into the shower,
toast and coffee then she's on the job all within the hour.
All day long the fax machines and telephones keep ringing
but when she has a break, she dreams of what the weekend's bringing.

From nine to five she's entrenched in a business state of mind
but as quitting time closes in, she's starting to unwind.
She thought this week would never end each hour went so slow.
Now, it's Friday night, she's feeling right, raring to go.

Dressed up in her party clothes and brand-new spike heel shoes
she heads toward the neon lights to lose her workday blues.
She's having dinner with some friends to start off the night
then it's finding bigger dance floors to look for mister right.

Another night's bit the dust; another weekend gone too fast.
Why don't the easy living times ever seem to last?
Sunday night, alone again, curled up in her easy chair.
Where is her mister right? She can't find him anywhere.

The alarm clock cuts into her dream. It's blue Monday again.
Breakfast. Shower. Grab umbrella. Head out in the rain.
The workday world won't go away. This morning's unforgiving.
She heads back to her corporate world to make a decent living.

Yes, she's a corporate lady, hiding little girl lost dreams.
Wearing masks to hide the fact she's much more than she seems.
Something old. Something new. Something borrowed. Something blue.
She still believes in fairy tales and hopes hers will come true.

The Dream and I

I

Baked in the summer of your heat,
frozen in your winter sleet,
wound into the hair you braided,
trapped inside the love that faded,
you skipped me like a shiny stone
and left me here to cry alone.

You were the dream I could not hold;
nor could I turn your heart to gold.
Baked inside a burnt-out fire
I now relinquish all desire
to live inside this frozen dream
where I am that which I least seem.

II

The frozen dream is thawing now.
I've come unshackled from my vow.
At last before your jaded eyes
I surface in my new disguise.
I dance inside your crumbling arms
and seize you victim to my charms.
You struggle but you can't escape
the choke of this emotional rape.

But I've always been a fool for love
burned by scorching stars above.
And I've always been a fool for you
although you can't help be untrue.
So, I'll burn inside your summer heat
and freeze inside your winter sleet
if I can spend just one more minute
wrapped in love's dream with you in it.

Silver Down Dream

Then

In the glitter and shine of silver, down dream
and a satin sheet torn and frayed at the seam,
we tossed and we turned on a blanket of bliss
hypnotized by passion's deep hungry kiss;
slipping and sliding on the spine of the rain,
riding love's rapids again and again.

One Day:

There were sailboats and ships on a lost horizon
and a hazy charade we could not keep our eyes on.
In the distance a hot lemon sun imploding;
up close in our hearts, our emotions exploding.

Now:

In the back retro-room of my messed-up mind
I rummage and search until I can find
my shadow world filled with stories and songs
where the lost part of us still somehow belongs.

Reliving the best memories from my past,
with a stiff shot of scotch I lift up my glass
and drink to the legacy of what I least seem
in the glitter and shine of a silver, down dream.

A Statue

An old guitar
with broken strings;

Music
with no score.

I stand
inside my loneliness,

a statue,
nothing more.

Tears

There are tears:

        impermanent tears
        that pool, drip, and slide down my face.

There are tears:

        permanent tears
        that neither time nor tide can erase.

The sun sleeps.
The moon wakes.
        The moon sleeps.
        The sun bakes.
                Heaven shakes.
                The earth quakes.

There are tears:

        unshed tears
        that burn inside their pain,
            torrential tears
            ice-cold like winter rain.
A man laughs.
A woman cries.
        A woman lives.
        A man dies.
            A lover leaves.
            A heart grieves.

Yes, there are tears

        and then …

            there are TEARS.

That Lost Yesterday

On a day reserved for yesterday's tears
I count on my fingers fair-weather friends
that have come and gone throughout the years.

Old memories and faces vie for attention.
They resurrect their sorrowful heads
from a maze of deeds too sordid to mention.

In the distance I hear a soft voice calling,
from the winter canyons of my heart,
reminiscent of December snow falling.

The wisdom that comes from a thousand mistakes
surrenders knowledge to imbue and impart
the essence of heartbreak and the sound it makes.

We walk, we run and sometimes we dance.
Sometimes we stumble and sometimes we fall
into the fell clutch of circumstance.

Creeping through fog at the edge of my mind
my name emerges. I hear someone call.
I feel a chill, turn around and I find

there's a melody playing a forgotten song;
but the rhythm and music just can't co-exist
and the lyrics and notes don't seem to belong.

And there's a lost yesterday I long to regain.
Sometimes I can glimpse it inside the dense mist
lying there in the dust, the tears and the pain …

that lost yesterday I long to regain.

Without You

If you've looked in a mirror
and seen no-one there,
then you've seen a picture

          of me
         without you.

If you've knocked on a door
and nobody answers,
then you've felt the way

         I feel
         without you.

If you look in your soul
you might still find me there,
standing alone

         and lost
         without you.

If you search through your heart
there might still be a chance
to save me from being

         me
         without you.

Nature

Fresh Fallen Snow

On a white satin blanket of fresh fallen snow
we set down our footprints row beside row.
Tomorrow there'll be no trace we were here.
Our footprints and laughter will have disappeared.

Behind a gossamer filmy drape
a mystical world begins to take shape
echoing through a desolate terrain
like the haunting sound of a phantom train.

The absence of bird sounds reverberates
in a cloyed timid silence that hesitates.
Hidden from sight are the tiny field mice
and the stream is held quiet in rocks turned to ice.

Whispers hang softly above the snow's glare
like soft misty kisses in the chilled air.
The glazed opaque sky is dimming to gray
as we watch the pale sun slide from the day.

Like a sugary eye closing its lid
the blurred twilight sky slips from the grid.
Neon stars sparkle like blue diamond fire
line dancing on an invisible wire.

Inside we're at peace in the warmth of the fire
wrapped in the deep embrace of desire.
Outside the world rests in a soft surreal glow
on a white satin blanket of fresh fallen snow.

Matchstick Men

The matchstick men stand on guard
in the green glow of God's backyard..

Deep inside this forest glade,
shafting through sunlight and shade
in full leafy salute
they stand resolute
whispering to branches on high
of snow covered days gone by.

The sunlight waxes and wanes
cascading in burnt amber chains,
caressing a velvet carpet of moss,
shining old bark to mahogany gloss.
New blades of grass burst forth and grow
in this sanctuary of green glow,
kissing nature's aura and essence
with flowered gifts and perfumed presents.

The matchstick men trade dreams of fame
and languish beneath a summer flame:
trees in the sunlight burning bright
until day meets the edge of night.

Then, lowers the guard
in God's green back yard.

In the forest castle of night's keep
The matchstick men have fallen asleep...

      f
        a
          l
           l
            e
              n
                  asleep.

Sundial

Beyond the shadow of a doubt,
behind the white light filtered out,
time plays tricks with idle minds.
A moment pauses then unwinds.

In shafts of pale and silken light
the moon skates on the edge of night
preparing breakfast for the dawn.
As darkness fades out in a yawn
the sleeping sun begins to rise
and covers up sky's starry eyes.

Sol shines on an old sundial,
wistful, lingering for a while;
counting daylight down to death
from first light to final breath;
before its glow is filtered out
beyond the shadow of a doubt.

Tree Whispers

Past the point of fascination,
swaying in wind's exultation,
leaves fall like crepe paper and wool ·
in the afterglow of Nature's pull.

Reflections glisten in sunshine
on water's repast turned to wine.
Light pools, spools, starts to unwind
a Chardonnay to cleanse the mind.

        And for a while the lake sighs and glistens;
        but all the while the tree whispers and listens.

Perchance an eagle may fly by.
A teardrop may fall from his eye.
Autumn leaves start to undress,
waiting for fall to confess
she's fallen prey to winter's charms
and seeks the comfort of his arms.

        And for a while the lake fills with tears;
        but all the while the tree whispers and hears.

I watch not sands in the hourglass;
nor care I for hours as they pass.
I lay with my ear pressed to a tear
In sacred silence praying I'll hear
your voice, though I know you won't return.
In icy flames of heartache, I burn.

        And for a while the lake in silence cries;
        but evermore the tree whispers and sighs.

Lavender Lady

The lavender lady's been left unattended.
She's become wounded and cannot be mended.
She sheds tears and cries in sync with the rain
in a pool bearing lost hope's echo and stain.

She was never a stranger to this hard rain,
this kindred sister of harsh sibling pain.
They've held hands through centuries passing
surviving the seasons and slowly amassing
quaint surreal treasures and trivial things
like cracked stone-age mirrors and crackerjack rings.

She had them tucked away safe in her bosom,
close to her heart so she couldn't lose them;
but somehow inside the passage of time,
in a careless moment of cloyed pantomime,
a rogue southern wind came calling and flattering.
They spilled from her torn blouse, sequins scattering.
She was robbed of her most precious possessions
and now no amount of heartfelt confessions
will bring her heart back to its genuine self:
This statue that fell from grace and God's shelf.

The cut of her chin portrays a small quiver.
Her vacuous eyes seem to shudder and shiver.
Excommunicated, lost and unblessed
her heart is now only an ache in her breast.
She sheds tears and cries in sync with the rain.
Her cheeks are chipped, weather beaten and stained.

The lavender lady's been left unattended,
fatally wounded … and cannot be mended.

Morning Has Broken

Morning has broken, like soft stained glass,
a rainbow of dewdrops over the grass.
The noise and the din of the world's kept at bay
as misty dawn beckons and wakes the day.

The marshland fog ebbs and slowly abates
rising like smoke rings toward heaven's gates.
From the sable lips of an angel's daughter
a soft misty kiss brushes the water.

On the glistening gleam of this water world,
wings tucked in gently yet tightly furled,
the lovely ducks paddle slowly in rings
as a cloud overhead wanders and swings
on the torn edge of a reluctant sun
chasing pale distant dreams on the run.

Silence reigns in ripples and swirls.
A world within a world slowly whirls.
A blanket of grey fog drifts through the sky.
The whisper of a lonely loon's cry.
The crunch of pebbles. The rustle of leaves
as Mother Nature rolls up her sleeves
breaking the morning on yonder pond,
kissing the leaves, the grass and the frond,
dressing the edge of a hallowed bog.
Inside the tall grass the croak of a frog.

A magic mirror appears in the pond;
then old wizard nature waves her wand
conjuring up serendipity
reflecting this moment's serenity.

Morning has broken to release the day.
See the ducks swim and the clouds sway!

Pink Moment

A green layered dream of a satin pink moment
awakens and whispers in a soft hushed foment.

This Tahitian overlay of deep glossy paint
nestled beside a house shoddy and quaint
floats and drifts into my line of vision,
and cuts through the day like a velvet incision
into the optic nerve of delight,
tickling the edge of fancy's flight;

In the crease and fold of this pastoral scene,
birdsong and rose petals dance and preen.

A fairy godmother's gold crested carriage,
carries babies breath to a floral marriage,
as suckling birds and genteel flowers
weave through the minutes, unlacing the hours
into the fragrance of green layered dreams,
spilling pale pink moments from their seams
to soothe fevered brows and aching hearts.
This is the healing power Nature imparts.

Neon Glow

Beyond the neon glow
lies a sky of pearl and snow
catching shadows as they fall
on sandy shoulders like a shawl.
A pink horizon of small hills
from a distant paintbrush spills
and nestles in this gentle mood
like a dove in coven brood.
A white flame washes at the edge
of the desert's surreal ledge,

I close my eyes. A film rolls and reveals
tombstones where the sun bends and kneels.
I see ghosts of the past; rusty wagon wheels.
A piece of lost history slowly steels
'cross the canvas of this new wild west
where sins committed are never confessed;
where lizard and eagle dare to nest
in a barren land of prayers unblessed.

The neon flickers but never fades
in this casino land of masks and charades.
The joker's disguised in mad masquerades
Cheating and cuffing the ace of spades
in a land of trickster's escapades.
Las Vegas dressed in Versace shades
ablaze in the glare of neon glow;
a castle keep of dice and show.

Shadows and ghosts ebb and flow
Fading in and out of the neon glow.

Night Shades

The shadows from the trees slice and ribbon through the park.
Twilight slips and falls into the outstretched arms of dark.
The colours of the flowers have dulled beneath the sky.
The moon on the horizon's a gleaming bright white eye.
The wandering night wind whispers secrets of past glory
as it snakes through shade and glade writing a new story.
Spokes of moonlight glittering in a spray of sequins
begin to cleanse the universe of her sordid sins.
The wind picks up a trifle more rustling through the trees.
The moon is waxing lower wrestling night onto it's knees.

And all the world is set aglow in this sacred place
that soothes like holy water splashed softly on the face.
The shades of night are manifold as they touch the ground
whispering from far away in echoes of soft sound,
harbouring the fresh stardust of antiquated days
as they twist and turn their heads in night's star dusted maze
to view a million new pathways leading to the core
where a trillion twilight nights have passed away before.

Like an ever changing bruise on the lip of time
strange and cosmic chanting voices try to sing in rhyme
within this gracious symphony played with tender score
locked inside a concert hall behind a velvet door.
Speaking in torn languages to angels who might listen
the night shades' tears are swept away nevermore to glisten.

As twilight crashes into the jagged edge of dark,
shadows from the night shades' eyes are ebbing from the park.

Sweet Dragonfly
(for Janet Kvammen)

Q-tip, popsicle stick which one can it be?
The Dragonfly lands on the stem so deftly
like a pilot holding the rudder of a plane
shafting through sunlight, careening on rain;
wings spanning centuries of poetry's lore,
washing dreams in from a distant shore.
A surreal painting, it calms me to the core.
Its sparkling wings shimmer in sequined beauty,
this silky sky pirate searching for booty.

It's the pure essence of true elegance,
a glorious insect of pre-eminence;
Majestically weaving through daylight's dream;
Changing dark clouds to bright whipping cream.

A glimmer of serenity, a glimpse of timelessness;
A slice of serendipity, an opaque wing's caress.

Fly away fly away sweet Dragonfly
on a wet wing and a soft velvet sigh.
I'll keep this dream and this tear in my eye
until you return, sweet Dragonfly.

Through Sun Drops and Dew

I will follow you
Through sun drops and dew.
Always time travelling,
Forever unravelling,
On seashores and sand
And love's golden strand
Where mate stays with mate
Fulfilling their fate.

Further I'll follow
descending death's hollow
to touch your silk wings
and climb rainbow strings
together in ascension
to heaven's vast dimension.

Wherever you go
above, or below,
I will be with you
through sun drops and dew;
in pearly moonbeams,
and butterfly dreams,
always ... following you.

White Water Rapids

The white water rapids, frothing and foaming.
The slick black rocks, moaning and groaning.
The west wind howling.
The wood jamb growling
like a wild rabid dog, chasing a log
down a slippery crack
on the river's back.

The white water rapids gurgle and scream
in the tight choke hold of man and machine.
An eagle flies by
with selective eye.
It swoops and dips, claws and wing tips,
diving and wishing
for old-time fishing.

Once long ago there were birch bark canoes,
totem poles, ponies and moccasin shoes
imprinting the shore;
But that was before
machinery and dredges tore down mountain ledges,
in this twilight noon
of things done too soon.

An eagle drifts across the sky.
A teardrop falls from his eye.

Once, there were birch bark canoes ...

This Tree

This tree has always been.
Through the ages she has seen
love's initials in her bark
where young lovers left their mark;
hearts entwined in sweet embrace;
sometimes tears upon love's face.
Through the sunshine and the rain,
tender moments still remain.

This tree has always been,
changing in her shades of green,
home to robin, wren and lark.
A sentinel in Queens Park.
Games and laughter, children playing
'Neath her watchful branches swaying;
she witnesses each smile and sigh,
stretching tall to touch the sky.

This tree has always been:
winter stark and summer sheen;
dressing up in shiny leaves,
watching them fall from her sleeves;
falling prey to autumn's charms,
nestling into winter's arms;
touched by raindrops and moonglow,
blanketed with flakes of snow;
and as the seasons whirl and spin,
she welcomes each one back again.

This tree has always been,
whispering to the wind unseen;

And oh ... the sights she's seen!

Summer's Gone

Summer's gone …

Autumn to fall
and then winter's pall.
Snow pelting down
on frozen ground.

Fall chases winter
into spring's dawn
sprinkling her dreams
with summer's song.

This winter chill
will melt and spill
into a crisp spring sky of blue
chasing a summer long overdue.

Summer's gone …
but not for long.

Moment in Time

A scented lilac dusk
falling, shawling, calling.
A forgotten aroma of musk
from earth's floorboards is crawling,
embracing each blade and leaf
that slumbers and rests beneath
a pastel sky canopy
as far as the eye can see.

This moment in time
shivers and streams
in soft satin rhyme
through circles of dreams.

But alas,
it must pass

Shadows fall on clover.
The pale blue sky clouds over:
Marks the end of day.
Turns gun metal gray.
Chases day away.

The lilac dusk dissipates
and the moment in time abates.

Eye in the Sky

The eye in the sky on high and ablaze
in the purple daze of a twilight haze
imprints invisible moments of bliss
signed and sealed with a midnight kiss.

The dark side accentuates the bright
in a pearl residue of refracted sunlight;
burning eternity into my sight,
making me small inside this night.

A distant echo of reverberation
is shaking gently on heaven's foundation,
forming new sounds for imagination;
some for excitement some for sedation.

In this glimmer and shine that lights up the night,
a shimmering new bride in silk gown of white
is marrying the stars to sky written dust
engraved on a starry Mona Lisa bust.

Creativity – imagination's child,
reared in freedom, is running wild
polishing stars in a renegade sky
scattering love with every sigh,
delighting the eye in the sky on high.

Autumn's Fall

The world continues spinning around.
The seasons change without a sound.
Spring to summer, summer to autumn.
The cool wind whispers of things to come:
blue skies tinged with shades of gray,
nature's magic on display
ready for it's race and chase
as autumn flees from winter's embrace.

The falling away of the leaves has begun.
They've outrun their season in the sun:
green to yellow, gold and red,
weary trees tucked in their bed.
Leaves are skipping down the street
dancing to October's beat.
Under a burnished sky of rust
the summer sun has turned to dust.

Tectonic seasons are slipping and sliding.
The warm south wind has gone into hiding.
Raindrops bump and grind the breeze
hypnotized by fall's strip tease.
Nature quickens her pulse and pace.
Autumn burns out in a fiery blaze.
Leaves disappear without a trace
As autumn falls into winter's embrace.

All the Colours Bleed Into One
(Ekphrastic poem written to painting of the same name by Janet Kvammen)

Flowers, in the attic spun,
watch twilight drip through blue.
When all the colours bleed into one
the truth comes shining through.

Beneath the brilliant flowers,
pale images emerge:
I see a world within a world.
My pulse begins to surge!
This world of mystery
beneath the orange and yellow
echoes ancient history
in whispers soft and mellow.

> *As it is above*
> *so it is below.*
> *It's just a different version*
> *of what we see and know.*

Through eternal hours
the flowers feed the earth;
and the roots feed the flowers,
from death to new rebirth.

As purple twilight ebbs and flows
patches of blue rest in repose
then all the colours bleed into one;
beneath a sleeping sun.

Dark

Riding Styx River

I stand at Styx River
aflame in a shiver
on the frost bitten edge
of a loose shaky ledge.
I didn't care or know
where the road would go
when we started the show.
We were foolhardy asses
wearing rose coloured glasses,
Looking back I can see
we weren't meant to be.
Hard times came along
and ruined our song.
Our hearts came unstrung
and the dance came undone.
Everything went wrong
and then… you were gone.

Now I'm riding Styx River
on a Babylon shiver.
I'm in a strange land
and I can't understand
people rasping in tongues
from old collapsed lungs.
Voices ring in my head
from the dead and undead.

On the loose shaky edge
of this frost bitten ledge
I'm tumbling down
in a vacuum of sound
into the abyss
of the body bliss
and the hot lusty kiss
on Babylon's lips,
aflame in a shiver
riding Styx River.

Sharma Lon

I dreamed of a mystical land in lost sea.
As I walked the shoreline of eternity,
waves danced with sand beneath my bare feet.
The scent of palm trees drifted to meet
me as I took my leave to Sharma Lon.

I rode the high crest of a tsunami wave
into a well disguised, decadent cave;
dark, darker, darkest, no turning back.
All light disappeared through a small crevice crack.
Of a sudden the sun, moon, and stars were gone.

Nearing the crevice I saw it expand.
I thought for a moment I'd glimpsed God's hand;
then a yellow clawed talon pulled back a black curtain.
Heaven was lost. Of this, I was certain.
In the corner a dark red ungodly light shone.

A gun metal boat with a cracked mast was tethered
to a rock jawed dock; its sails torn and weathered.
A clawed hand grabbed my arm. I was led to her side
to travel blood's river where chained ghosts abide
deep inside dreaded Sharma Lon.

The boat moaned and groaned with guttural grind.
Death, rage, destruction began to unwind
in film noir clip resurrected to life,
reeling with temptation, war, tears and strife;
innocent faces turned ghostly and wan.

Down the back of my neck, hot fetid breath dripped.
Inside a damp fog a dead carcass hung ripped.
A voice spewing danger, warned me as we passed
of Hell's lake of fire where my soul would be cast
into endless night with no rumour of dawn.

Screams and moans rose in velocity.
I witnessed agony's atrocity:
A man being flayed on a barbed wire tree.
Demons, deriding, and mocking me.
Ghastly, maimed mimics in wild abandon.

A sudden explosion exposed carnal sin
in a strange madrigal of lost yang and yin.
A mad king's sword stabbed a Queen's heart of tin.
Nude boys and naked maids frolicked within
and lined the bleak alleys of Sharma Lon.

Skeletons once clothed in flesh, hung by bone
on a rusted bell tolling in ear-piercing tone.
An Incubus suckled a young demon soul.
A worm squirmed out from an eye socket hole.
No angels dared enter feared Sharma Lon.

A red demon devil with black charcoal eyes,
from Lucifer's fiery pit, began to rise.
Spectre with sceptre, the Trident of Hell,
prince of dark kingdoms and bastards pell-mell,
ruling in Hades where light never shone.

Red poison was poured. I was handed the vial.
I forced my eyes closed in hope of denial.
Then suddenly hovering over my head,
a masked ghoul and trident with blood of the dead.
My skull was to decorate Sharma Lon.

I begged for a reprieve, said I'd do anything,
and then in one fell swoop a horrendous sting.
The sharp gleaming Trident pierced skull, heart and gut.
The harsh pain and agony woke me up.
Beads of sweat, wet the welcoming dawn.

In the arms of the angels, alive and awake,
I ride on their wings and feel heaven shake.

The mystical nightmare I dreamed of is gone;
swallowed up inside an angel's yawn,
buried and gone, dreaded Sharma Lon.

Forever buried and gone …
Sharma Lon.

The Depth of Her Fall

White time cracked
Building to black
Raindrops unstacked
Clouds come untacked
From weakened sky
In secretive lie
The lure of the lonely
Touching one only
In gossamer nightgown
Without throne or crown
A satin doll
In the crest of her fall
Barely alive
But she will survive
Atmospheres, alters
Horses, thrown halters
Saddled up for the ride
Through eternal tide
Tears polished to shine.
Breath flavoured with wine
Sweet inebriation
Seeking expiation
This deep black chasm
Tick-tocking spasm
Holds court every night
Squeezes the light
Into lost works of art
Painted for her dark heart
Torn dreams on parade
In dull masquerade
Winter wind through the soul
From unblessed hell hole
Chasing her to the edge
On precarious ledge
Now back to the wall
Soon she will recall
The depth of her fall.

13th Cusp

At the edge of the thirteenth cusp's bag of tricks
I cling to the shore of the River Styx.
Barbed wire bony fingers claw flesh from my soul.
The edge of night lingers as dark as black coal
inside this painting of hellish perdition.
There's nowhere to end and no place to begin
begging for contrition in a galaxy too far.
I smell ancient battle, and blood on a scar
in the damp cicatrix of apocalypse
dead on arrival rancid blood drips from lips.
Hanging on the edge of stale breath bated,
Satan's on the prowl, his hunger unsated.

Horned ravens suckle on death's fetid breath;
in hot lava, burnt flesh and creeping death.
Riveted and writhing in a dark bat-winged curtain,
the blind clutch the blind, shaken, fearful and uncertain,
tearing out their eyeballs in fear of second sight,
stumbling on dismembered limbs at the edge of night.
They're lost in this darkness, these emaciated foes
as Lucifer swallows their souls' fleeing shadows.

On the 13th cusp, I stand balanced perfectly
as death's delivery table rebirths reality.
Cloaked in superstitions and mired in dark fears
I become the blood of invisible tears.

My heartbeat is failing. The saber has been thrust.
Bleeding out in blackest night, I am the 13th cusp.

A Murder of Crows

The night unzipped a bloodstained rose
and spilled tears from its ebony jar.
The sky came alive with a murder of crows.
It cracked at the seams and broke to expose
the jagged saw-edge of a shattered star
as the night unzipped a bloodstained rose.
The essences, ember-prints and afterglows
of pulsating dead sparks became a hot scar;
and the sky came alive with a murder of crows.
Like a charcoal mist on December snows
this dream was sullied and always too far.
The night unzipped a bloodstained rose
with fragile arrows and broken bows.
In the wounded paw of a raging jaguar
The sky came alive with a murder of crows.
My cup ran over, then shattered and froze.
As I stepped back into my avatar
the night unzipped a bloodstained rose;
and the sky came alive with a murder of crows.

Street of Long Shadows

I walk alone in darkness on the dim street of long shadows.
A haunting cold hard evil slowly crests then ebbs and flows.
Inside this mist a fog approaches, and starts to creep around me.
I'm touched by icy fingers and opaque figures I can't see.
As goose flesh rises up on the cold nape of my neck
I turn around in fear and scan the empty street to check
for ghostly strangers in the mist who want to do me harm.
I feel a bony hand clawing at my chest and arm.
I hear a distant moaning murmur on the path ahead
inside this night of terror that reeks of death and dread.

Approaching me with glowing eyes are thirteen demon cats
and overhead cacophonies of rabid screeching bats.
A devil with sharp horns chasing me begins to gain.
Ahead a ghoulish vampire is waiting in the lane.

Paranoia's madness unravels at the seam
as hungry demons chew through the edges of this dream
but this is not a nightmare. It's real and I'm awake.
There's no escape from bedlam, no other road to take.
I hear a distant ring of angels clamouring for my sake.
But they're still too far away to do battle at my side.
I feel the crush of gnashing teeth and static flesh collide.
Now paralyzed, I cannot move and wonder if I've died.
It's then I finally realize my body's passed away.
I rise in vapor and become a misty shape of gray.
Co-joined with cold hard evil as it ebbs and flows,
I am a darkened shadow on the dead street of long shadows.

Ashmodai Garden

And all the white in the world couldn't save her
from the heartache and woe the archangel gave her.
She screamed from the top of her lungs; but in vain.
She was lost to this world; she'd been driven insane.

And all the dark soil in the Ashmodai garden
seeped into her heart and caused it to harden.
The agony etched deep into her face
reflected the depth of her fall from grace.

As she sunk slowly down in a dark soggy grave
the devils and demons were filled with the crave
for this meal of spilled blood as she started to die
in the bastardized garden of dark Ashmodai.

There's no chance of redemption. She'll always lie
in the bastardized garden of dark Ashmodai.

Princess of the Tower

There's a man-bear on the floor and a damsel on the bed
and a wolf at the door that's howling to be fed.

The man-bear comes out of his animal disguise
and feeds hungrily on the passion in her eyes.
He moves with deliverance from his loosened bearskin
burning with a fever and fire deep within.
He crawls, then he walks, then her crawls once again
in perilous tandem with his grief and his pain,
seeking his vainglorious hour of power
making love to the princess of the tower.

He bridles and sidles like a wild stallion horse
at odds with his passion's demonic force.
He's always out of sync with his grizzly bear roots.
He's a numberless number that never computes.
He's the answer to an IQ test that has no score.
He's the secret that whispers behind a closed door.

He slowly approaches his quarry, his prey;
his lover, his mistress in this ungodly play.
The walls close in on her attempts at escape.
She's the sweet sweating victim of consensual rape.
He can smell her surrender envelop the room
as she willingly welcomes the bliss of her doom.

Ibbur

A teddy-bear girl sits on a bed of warm fleece
and submerges herself in the books open crease.
She reads and she seeds 'til she conjures a dream
and revives soiled toys she hopes to redeem.

Stirring new stories in an old rusty cup
she chants magic rituals as her essence climbs up
from the demonic land of fire and hot coals
to the land of transmigration and righteous souls.

There are highways and roads; some are passed by, some taken.
Opportunities come knocking; some are answered, some forsaken.
There's a reckoning and four pathways at each intersection;
and a myriad of star-crossed souls seeking direction.

In each wasted life there's always something positive;
and for each one well-lived there's always something negative.
Tenets and beliefs are raked over the coals
as Dybbuk and Ibbur do battle for souls.

Personification, impregnation, occupation,
esoteric, ethereal intrepid incarnation.
It's here in this blurred world and it's over there.
It's the visible invisible and it's everywhere.

So, back to the little girl sitting on her bed
with the dark curls of conscience flowing from her head.
This teddy-bear child is awake and astir
with the knowledge of life, afterlife and Ibbur.

She's been here before and she'll be here again.
She's mind, soul and body in sun, wind and rain.
She's sea, sky and spirit; she's love, hope and pain.
She's life, death and Ibbur's indelible stain.

Eerie Shadowlands

In eerie shadow lands I lurk and hide.
I am a hellish pawn, the devil's pride.
A midnight monster hunting flesh and blood,
the greedy essence of your worst nightmare.
Slowly flaying back raw skin and bone
I'll strip your skeleton and conscience bare.
I'll crush you to the sharp knives in my chest.
I am the taker of dark souls un-blest.

On any darkened foggy eerie night
I'm always near but hiding out of sight
in seedy alleys where I wait to pounce
and drink your tasty blood to the last ounce.
And when the savory meal at last is done
I chase the moon and then outrun the sun.

I am the undead angel bringing death,
A ghoulish vacuum sucking your last breath.
I am a hellish pawn, the devil's pride.
In eerie shadow lands I lurk and hide.

Escape

Always on guard and ever vigilant
he sees the edge of darkness closing in.
He's locked in shadows cold and indigent
and shackled to Pandora's box of sin.
He hears the rattle of skeletal bones.
They clamour, echoing incessantly;
in atmospheres alive with curdled moans
that claw with tooth and nail to be set free.
Inside this prison cell of insurrection
are blatant deeds too horrible to mention.
This bony ghost is death's last resurrection.
His keychain rattles and demands attention.

His eyes slam shut. His keys fall to the floor.
He can't escape. He's trapped behind death's door.

Further From The Light

A darkened satyr comes to me at night
disguised as gargoyle in gun metal gray
and I am taken further from the light.
All is blackness not a trace of white
in this abyss where there's no trace of day.
A darkened satyr comes to me at night
wings shackled so there is no chance of flight;
lips sealed shut there are no words to say
and I am taken further from the light.
Blood seeping from teeth as they gnash and bite
I close my eyes and I begin to pray.
A darkened satyr comes to me at night.
I hope an angel will assuage my plight.
I've lost my hope somewhere along the way
and I am taken further from the light.
The corners of this prison now grow tight.
Grotesque figures in the moonlight sway.
A darkened satyr comes to me at night
and I am taken further from the light.

Leaving the Past Behind

They whisper, they coo, and they call
from their derelict side of the wall.
They push forward to peer through a crack.
They watch as she's turning her back
on wasted nights and a sordid past.
They can't believe the die has been cast.
She's given her notice and finally resigned.
She's leaving the past behind.

They whine, and they crawl, and they bawl
from their cold lonely side of the wall;
and all their sad crocodile tears
can never erase the bad years.
They mocked, they tortured and taunted;
made her feel unloved and unwanted.
Then one day she made the choice
to silence their abusive voice.
She turned it around. She's now redefined.
She's leaving the past behind.

They slip, slide, stumble and fall
on their ice-riddled side of the wall.
They furiously try to make her stay
but she doesn't look back as she's walking away
She sees them at last as they truly are:
The self-effaced dust of a burnt-out star.
A horrendous cut of a blood curdling scream
trying to destroy her and her dream.
But she's no longer weak, frail and blind,
She's leaving the past behind.

Ghostly Tryst

Rhiannon's ghost lurks in the moor's cloyed mists.
The champing steed is quiv'ring in alarm.
The horseman grips the reins with tightened fists.
He draws his sword to ward off pending harm.
It glistens bright in shafts of pearl moonbeams.
An ancient lost marauder's heart of steel,
is trapped in claws of lust's recurring dreams.
A madness spins eternity's wild wheel.
Rhiannon snares him in her cold embrace.
Her ghostly, teeth sink deep into his bone.
Time disappears reversing inner space.
Old embers turn to ashes; hearts to stone.

Beneath a devil sky, star crossed, moon kissed,
The witch and horseman dance in ghostly tryst.

Psychosis

Inside this darkened paradigm of doom
harsh paranoia's zealot speaks in tongues.
Damp ghostly whispers drown this floating room.
I climb frail ladders rife with broken rungs.
My ears crack with the high pitched screech of bats.
Dark spectres chase me through horrific nights
past frowning clowns in corners changing hats
and sad gorillas chasing tattered kites.
Enveloped in high frequency white noise
ghosts stand in stoic silence by my bed.
Death's lost its sting and I have lost my voice
and now I walk alone amongst the dead.
Their hearts are hard as steel, eyes black as coal;
they rend and shred the essence of my soul.

Shadow People

The downtown east side streets scream out in pain
in heavy-hearted breath, in hollow voice.
Hard desperation's drowning in the rain,
where shadow people live without a choice.
They're strewn and scattered broken bowling pins.
They litter alleys in haphazard spill.
They search for food and clothes in garbage bins.
A cardboard box their shelter in life's swill,
they try to find the crumbling edge of sleep.
They chase their shadows past the point of light,
these broken Cinderellas in too deep;
these torn Prince Charmings zipped inside the night.

Inside the cold clutch of fell circumstance,
these shadow people never have a chance.

Stale Bled Scar of Life

Oozing dark, dank fear and strife
from the stale bled scar of life,
the fresh cut spirit from the flesh
in ghostly form, askew, enmeshed,
claws at holes that once held eyes
now bereft of all disguise.

Deep inside destruction's hold
forgiveness can't be bought or sold.
Lucifer, in ghastly robes
beneath a flame that spins and strobes,
pins minions to his broken cross
where sinners' souls lay torn and tossed.
Inside the cauldron of fire's hell
on hollow waves that moan and swell.
walls drip with bloodstains manifold
in fire emblazoned frozen cold.

That one could be cast to this fate,
forever in ungodly state
is cruelty one can't comprehend;
eternal torture without end.

These sinners rue the choice they made.
They left the light to walk in shade.
Sordid deeds left unconfessed
remain a testament unblessed.
They ooze dark fear and echo strife
from the stale bled scar of life.

The Whistler

The whistler wanders graveyards late at night.
and hums a haunting eerie melody.
He hides in shadows cast by fading light.
A threat'ning figure skulking murd'rously,
he feigns non sequiturs, so sweet and low.
He lures lost, wounded souls into his snare.
His victims line death's doorway row on row.
A dangerous acquaintance should fools dare
to grasp his hand when lost in creeping fog.
He chews their mem'ries, dining on their soul;
this mascot straight from Hell, a demon dog,
with heart as dark as night; eyes black as coal.
The whistler hides in corners of the night.
He cannot touch those walking in the light.

History
&
Story

The Hanging Judge

Judge Matthew Baillie Begbie lived in New Westminster from 1860 to 1870. He was Chief Justice of all British Columbia in 1870. Knighted in 1875, he retained his position until his death on June 11, 1894. His total tenure on the B.C. bench was 36 years. His name remains a cornerstone in B.C. history.

Outside the New West courthouse there looms a large statue,
a man bound by integrity, steadfast, strong and true.
In 1858 he came to shape our history.
They called him the hanging judge, Sir Matthew Baillie Begbie.
His influence was felt far and wide across the land.
His statue stands impressive, big and tall like the man.

Bearded and 6 foot five, he was a daunting presence.
A "justice for all" spirit, accompanied each sentence.
The wild west, gold rush era was a shrewd outlaw's delight
'til Begbie's law arrived in town to teach them wrong from right.
He walked or rode on horseback to the outback settlements.
In British wig and black hat, he heard cases in his tent.
He used the law and used the noose to tame this great province.
He was a man of morals, born and raised by Providence.

During fourteen years on the bench as magistrate,
twenty-seven men were hanged and kept their date with fate.
A bronze sculpted statue standing seven feet tall
is a tribute to the hanging judge who answered duty's call;
Sir Matthew Baillie Begbie, harsh, stern, austere, yet fair.
A monument to this great man once stood in Begbie Square

Judge Begbie, originally was called the "Haranguing Judge" as he was prone to scold convicted felons before passing sentence. Over the years he has erroneously become known as "The Hanging Judge" even though his record shows that he was a very merciful judge compared to others of his era

Ghosts of the BC Penitentiary

(The BC Penitentiary was British Columbia's main prison, situated in the heart of New Westminster, BC overlooking the mighty Fraser River, from 1876-1980)

On the old Pen property spirits lurk and hide.
Ghostly voices whisper in the pale moonlight.
A heavy door slams shut with a thunderous clap.
A frayed noose hangs above a floor trap,
And yesterday's ghosts still walk these grounds at night.

Built in 1878 she was a fortress strong,
a bleak home for felons who did the law wrong.
Her tall cement walls loomed large inside our town.
This daunting human cage never let her guard down.
She stood at full attention an ominous landmark,
foreboding, gray and dark, harsh and stern and stark.

As a youngster I remember Cumberland Street.
On hot sultry days, sweating bullets in the heat
the prisoners in groups and gangs laboured in the yard
lined up in the sights of the tower guns and guards.
The murderer and thief toiled side by side.
With leg irons and secrets, they were tethered and tied.

1976 was the Pen's worst riot date.
The east wing was destroyed in this meeting with fate.
In the aftermath she was scheduled for tear down.
She'd overstayed her welcome in our residential town.

She closed in 1980 on the 10th day of May.
But, listen to my words and hear me when I say ...

On the old BC Pen property spirits lurk and hide.
Ghostly voices whisper in the pale moonlight.
AND...Yesterday's ghosts STILL walk these grounds at night !.

THX 1138

THX-eleven thirty-eight
can you please tell me of my fate?
Do we all have 3 paths we can travel?
Can we choose how our days will unravel?

Are we all born with the same potential?
Is there no such thing as co-incidental?
Is each person we meet along the way
somehow instrumental in our private play?

Who decides which folks are very important?
Why can't we know who will prove discordant?
Do we choose our parents or do they choose us?
Why do some babies laugh and others fuss?

Why do some friends stay while others must go?
Why are there some answers we cannot know?
Why are some honest and why do some cheat?
Do we all have missions we must complete?

Why do some speak gently while others cuss?
Why do some ride limos, others a bus?
Some are gravediggers and some engineers,
but we are all equal when death appears.

THX eleven thirty-eight
I don't really want to know my fate.
I'll just go day by day as they unravel.
I hope I choose the right path to travel.

Some things belong behind lips tightly sealed
and some things are better left … unrevealed.

BURRARD DRYDOCK DAYS
(Memories told to me by Ken Ader)

I was what you'd call a dumb welder, workin' for a livin';
a hard drinkin' man wantin'all the world was givin'.
Sweatin' at Burrard Drydocks, 1973 to 90,
I knew my way around real good. The boss could never find me.

At Burrard Drydocks, sweatin' heavy dirt and grime,
some of the things we done - it was almost a crime.
When deadlines were loomin' we were under the gun
so we'd jerk on old Bill's chain just to have a little fun.
Old Bill worked the bull gang and sometimes the service pool,
settin' staging, movin' planks, but he never used a tool.
He was a worn out work horse gettin' ready to retire,
but some of us guys could still light his ass on fire.
Bill did all the clean up and stockin' of the washroom,
dredgin' a bucket mop and pushin' an old broom.
We had a special name for him and as I do recall
we called him Shithouse Bill cause he put rumours on the wall.

We'd tell old Bill a crazy lie and say "Don't tell a soul.
Keep your yappy trap shut. Don't open your cakehole."
To start a red hot rumour runnin' wild and goin' 'round
we'd just tell it to old Bill then put our ear to the ground.
I once told Bill a big repair was comin' up.
Said we might finish in a week with a little luck
Said there'd be some overtime and dirty money too
when all the job needed was a shit, shave and shampoo;
some paint, sandblast, and water sweep to wipe away the grime;
in truth no bonus for this job, for sure no overtime.
Then when the rumour bit the dust Bill laughed as much as us.
He loved a bit of turnabout a chance to strut and cuss.

I'm long retired for years now but every once in a while
I think about old Shithouse Bill and break into a smile.
That tough old guy could bring a tear to a glass eye.
My days at Burrard Drydocks still live inside my mind,
and Shithouse Bill is still a favourite memory of mine.

Peril Keep

"Aye laddie, off yer arse and swab the bloody deck.
Swab it once then swab it twice. I'll be back to check.
Use muscle, spit and polish. Make the '*Sea Queen*' shine like gold.
If I find a speck o' dirt ye'll be snorin' in the hold.

I runs a tight ship always, even tighter on the main.
I've locked horns with wilds beasts that were the devil's bane
and if ye think ye'll outsmart me yer dumber than ye look.
I've got yer number, pirate boy, written in me book.

If ye mess with the bearded man that wears the Cap'n's hat,
ye'll feel ten o' the nine tails snap from the leather cat.
But if yer deed be dastardly I'll make ye walk the plank.
Ye can bet yer boots on that me lad like money in the bank.

I've sailed the seven seas and then a wee bit more.
I've always been a savage man that settles every score.
500 men have crossed me, boy, and they be dead as doors;
some scoundrels beggin' fer their lives, crawlin' on all fours.

But I be not bent to sentiment or sympathy at all.
500 men had drawn their swords. 500 men did fall.
Remember Long John Silver and old Blackbeard his'self?
I sent 'em down with fatal wounds to Davy Jones' shelf.

So now we be at sea for twenty seven days and one,
searchin' for a sea dog breeze in this rabid Sun.
But don't lose heart my bra' young tar, I smell me treasure near.
Just around that jut of land an island will appear.

Many a tar heel's lived and died tryin' to find me gold.
Many a map's been spattered with blood and torn along the fold.
The only ones that knows the cave is me and peg leg Fred
And many a moon has come and gone since peg leg Fred's been dead.

So, I's the only one that knows the course we has to steer.
We'll crack that chest and hold the gold and hoist a cup o' cheer.
Har! Look I see the Sun's come up and brought a breeze to boot.
The cook will still be sleepin', lad. Go rustle that old coot.

And while you're at it boy, rouse the wretches from their bed.
Once we've filled our guts with grits we'll sail full speed ahead
to the cave of plenty where we'll share and share alike.
But Cap'n gets a bit more for his sailin' ship and strike."

The ship did heave. The ship did shudder as they braved the waves
that tossed and turned the ship above old pirates in their graves.
Then round the jut of land they came and the sea became a lake;,
placid and inviting them to come and grab their take.

"Thar' she be boys, shinin' like a diamond in the deep.
A fortune in gold's buried in the cave of Peril Keep.
So down the boats and man the oars and row hard fer the shore.
Waitin' there, fer us, is gold doubloons, and jewels and more.

That rocky grey faced opening's a sight for these sore eyes.
Inside its jaw then two left jogs be where me treasure lies.
Ye'll get your fair share that's fer sure, the cut won't be lopsided.
So when we gets there mind yer manners til the pot's divided."

And so this motley crew debarked and dug with haste and speed.
In great anticipation their eyes grew wide with greed.
At last they heard the welcome clunk of wood and clang of steel.
They brought the chest up to the top and broke the lock and seal.

The glare of gold did glitter. Diamonds and rubies shone.
They shared the loot and drank the boot until the crack of dawn.
Then Black Bart, with blackguard heart, said "I deserve some more";
his pistol aimed at Captain Cord, but a shot rang out before

Black Bart could pull the trigger. Billy plugged him 'tween the eyes.
Black Bart fell dead upon the floor, face frozen with surprise.
The deck hand Billy Bob was now the hero of the day.
The Captain's fair haired laddie had made that devil pay!

The Captain and his motley crew can sometimes still be seen
gliding through the waters on the waterlogged '*Sea Queen*'.
The ghosts of Billy Bob and Captain Cord still sail the deep,
wandering the waters near the cave of Peril Keep.

Sacrosanct Shade

I danced on the edge of a Tsunami wave,
tripping and falling into a dark cave;
as I lost my last grasp on consciousness,
Spirits unwrapped in full state of undress.

Waking up in a suffocating heat,
head swimming in pain with every pulse beat,
I find a match and proceed to light it.
On the walls, stone age paintings. Fear grabs me. I bite it.

From behind me hushed voices, now growing loud.
A motley crew, ancient ones, round me did crowd
They drew me into an aura of blue.
On a misty cloud, through the paintings we flew.

Blinded by white light we sped through the air.
When we alit all I could do was stare.
I gazed upon acres of velvet green grass;
all types of wildlife gathered en masse.

All communication was delivered by thought.
I knew their strange language without being taught.
They bade me follow them through a forest glade
where elf and fawn frolicked in velvet green shade.

Strange magical music permeated the air.
Feelings of joy and love were everywhere.
The sun never set. The moon always hung high.
Embraced in the breath of a soft surreal sigh.

Everything happened now. Time did not pass;
there was only this moment of sweet demi tasse.
The wine was the color of magenta grape.
I sipped as the music and dancers took shape.

A vision of beauty and sanctified sound
filled up my mind and began to surround
every wish I had ever tried to lay claim to.
They were magically conjured up then they came true.

I noticed my body was now supple and lean.
Energized, I felt like I was nineteen.
A beautiful spirit took me by the hand
and danced me through rainbows in this wonderland.

The sky shed raindrops of deep azure blue.
Everything shone in their sparkling dew.
I knew I was born for a moment like this
that melts the heart with the cool of a kiss.

In the blink of an eye there was born a blue lake;
and it was created that I may forsake
each trepidation, heartache and fear.
It erased, from my soul, every pain and each tear.

On gossamer wings I flew light as a feather.
Then on the horizon, a change in the weather;
a hushed hazy whisper passed through the throngs.
They gathered in gospel chanting strange songs.

The air began circling in soft undulation
then grew thick and heavy with great expectation.
The lake harnessed me in her Tsunami wave
and covered me in a soft watery grave.

Lost in deep sleep for I know not how long,
I awoke all alone; my sweet captors gone.
But the dream was real, bed sheets crumpled; still wet
with the blue of that lost lake I'll never forget.

Now each night I search for a Tsunami wave
to carry me back to that magical cave:
to the green forest glade where elf and fawn played;
to the crystal blue lake and that sacrosanct shade.

Elijah

Elijah … A high priest in biblical history;
an extremely complicated prophet of mystery.

Bearded in white robe, a barefoot figurine;
a participant, a witness and someone in between,
he illuminates salvation in a room filled with candles
behind padlocked doors that have broken handles.

He's seen angels' wings ripped from the bosom of love
and watched as their torn feathers fell from above.
Elijah can't speak to souls lost by the wayside.
His mouth's been sealed closed to stem his truth's tide.

So, he continues to light sacred candles each night
hoping angels that have been lost in flight,
or caught in a dark storm's harsh ebb and flow,
will find their way home in the bright candle glow.

He's Archangel Sandalphon of music and sacrament.
He's Elijah the revered "Angel of the Covenant".

Cowboy
Poetry

The Outlaw Billy Miner

Back in the 1880s the outlaw Billy Miner
was either breaking the law or breaking out of jail.
Up in these parts in the City of New Westminster
he did time in the B.C. Pen for robbing CP Rail.

Bill spent some time in New York in the social climbing game.
Dressed up in a three-piece suit he used different name.
When his cash supply was gone back out west, he came.
An outlaw riding through the land was his claim to fame.

He held up stages in the states and trains in Canada,
always travelling with a gun and running from the law.
There never was a prison that could hold him very long.
He'd find a way to break out and then he'd be long gone.

In 1904 Canada's first train robbery
was pulled off by Bill Miner making history.
He held up the C.P.R. with outlaw Shorty Dunn.
Ten thousand worth of gold and bonds put them on the run.

Again in 1906 he robbed the C.P.R. in May.
In June he was sentenced to a lifetime prison stay.
He stood in court and told the judge *"No jail can hold me sir."*
In August of the next year he'd back up his word.

He broke out of the B.C. Pen in 1907;
and was back in jail in Georgia by spring 1911.
He busted out of Georgia pen two more times and then,
in this life here on earth he never escaped again.

On September 2nd, 1913 Billy Miner drew his final breath
and made his last escape in the arms of the angel of death.

Silver Spurs a-Jinglin'

With silver spurs a-jinglin' he walked into the bar.
He had a glittering eye and a weathered jagged scar.
It ran the length of his cheek and up into his hair.
Jake had that kind of look like he'd been everywhere.

He set down in the corner his back against the wall.
Even sittin' down this cowboy sat really tall.
He pulled a deck of cards and started shufflin' them around.
The ace of spades fell face up when it hit the ground.

A stranger in black boots stepped his right foot on it.
His face looked like a puzzle with pieces that don't fit.
He kicked the card and challenged Jake to some six-gun poker.
The ace of spades was gonna place a bet against the joker.

Now everybody knows the joker is the top wild card
and when it's played against an ace the chips fall fast and hard.
The stranger drew his six-gun faster than the eye
but Jake was like greased lightning; the stranger had to die.

The stranger's body lurched then fell dead on the floor.
Jake gathered up the cards and shuffled them once more.
He pulled just one card out and put the rest aside.
He threw the ace of spades down where the stranger lie.

With silver spurs a-jinglin' Jake walked into the street.
The night was hot and muggy and had a deathly heat.
He climbed in his saddle and wiped sweat from his head,
then pulled his hat down low and thought about the dead.

Midnight Shoot Out

Platinum sheet lightning lit up the lone prairie.
A midnight shoot-out film played in the sky above me.
I heard a lone wolf howling a chilling haunting song
and then across the sky I saw ten riders riding strong.

The thundering of the horses hooves echoed thru the night
as I bore silent witness to this blurred and ghostly sight;
five Hatfields on the left and five McCoy boys on the right
were mounted on their wild -eyed stallions, guns drawn for a fight.

The tall scar-faced outlaw riders had hatred in their eyes.
The midnight sky was lit up like a blazing hot sunrise.
Their horses were pale phantoms, snorting foggy breath,
carrying ghosts riders in a sky that screamed of death.

I heard Anse Hatfield's voice blurt out "McCoy! This is your last;
You won't ride this range again" and then I heard a blast.
Ole Ran was hit in the chest, but dead men's ghosts don't fall.
Already dead, he couldn't die and so he still rode tall.

Then the midnight sky became a deadly quiet clear.
There was no noise at all in the hazy atmosphere.
I relit my campfire to burn off the ghostly chill
and thought about dead men and ghosts and reasons why men kill.

Bad Day in Red Deer

The sun was beating down, 'bout a hundred & ten degrees.
Even the dogs were sweating, passed out in the streets.
You could smell trouble in the air.
You could feel it everywhere.
It was a bad day in Red Deer. It was worse than the heat.

I was sippin' whiskey down, at the Red Dog Saloon,
tryin' to quench a powerful thirst like all the rest were doin'.
The boys were playin' pay cards.
The stakes were high and hard.
When we heard the first shots, it was just about high noon.

We heard the women screamin', and we hit them swingin' doors.
The sheriff he'd been hit hard and was crawlin' on all fours.
Our guns were drawn and ready.
Our hands were sure and steady,
and then I saw Jess Carter's face. He was settlin' old scores.

Now Jesse he'd once saved my life so I couldn't gun him down.
Then Jesse's eyes met mine as his gun hand spun around.
In that one split second,
before either of us reckoned,
a bullet from another gun drove Jesse to the ground.

I dodged through the gunfire and ran where Jesse lay.
Old memories came rushing back of kid's play yesterday.
Jesse'd fenced with death
and death took his last breath.
I bit my lip to stop the tears as Jesse slipped away.

I turned and walked away, shaky in the knees,
thinkin' 'bout the carnage layin' back there in the street.
I wiped the sweat from my head
and said a prayer for the dead.
It was a bad day in Red Deer. It was worse than the heat.

Bringin' 'Em In

It's rough out on the trail of a cattle drive.
Some wranglers make it. Some don't come back alive.
Some die from the heat. Some die from the herd.
Some just die from heartache, but they don't say a word.

And out on the trail…

You head for the watering hole, the one you used before,
but now she's dry as a bone and sunburnt to the core.
Your canteen is empty and your throat's dry and hot.
You shake it for the water you know it hasn't got.

So you keep driving the cattle up around the next bend
but still there ain't no water; just desert without end.
You're startin' to cough and wretch. You know you're in deep trouble.
Your head's gettin' heavy and you're startin' to see double.

And just when you're thinkin' you ain't got a chance,
it's wet on your forehead as the rain starts to dance.
It pours down in torrents and you laugh and jump for joy
and just for a moment you feel like a little boy.

The rain keeps pourin' down and you watch the puddles form.
The cattle are a quiet bunch in this summer storm.
They're soaked to the skin and their tongues are cold and wet.
These clouds are a long-lost friend you never will forget.

Yeah, it's tough out on the trail drivin' cattle to a sale,
eatin' when you can and drinkin' water that's gone stale.
Sure the pay is good and most of the time you win
but the biggest thrill of all is just *'bringin' 'em in'* !

The Smell of Death and Dead Men

It was an hour before sunset and the sun was hangin' red.
The posse and the outlaws were packin' steel and lead.
Some would walk away that day and some would fall there dead.
Those that bit the dust that day would have a Boot Hill bed.

I was just twelve years old, green and scared as hell.
I crouched down and hid behind the old abandoned well.
I watched them kickin' up the dust that motley outlaw hoard.
I saw each man's gritty stare before the gunfire roared.
The battle, short and bloody, settled up the score.
Men who'd lived and breathed, would live and breathe no more.

The gun smoke slowly cleared, and the street was safe again.
Pools of blood mixed with dust beside the fallen men.
I rushed into the crowded street that oozed the smell of death.
The air was thick and sour. I had to gasp for breath.
I was searchin' with a bad feelin' for my brother Bill.
I hoped he'd still be alive, if it was God's will.

Then I saw Bill layin' there, all still and turnin' gray.
I ran fast to his side, knelt down, began to pray;
but Bill had been shot dead and blood was on the moon,
and them that was still livin' went back to the saloon.

It's been a real long time since that deathly day.
But in my mind the carnage will never fade away.

Sometimes late at night
I recall that day and then,
I swear I smell that sickly smell…
the smell of death and dead men.

Lone Run

The gleaming silver and black iron horse
thundered down the virgin track,
puffing and steaming with magnum force,
burning and churning black smoke from her stack.
Through the renegade land of the Navajo
smoke signals painted the sentinel sky.
The dark iron horse kicked and grunted below
snaking up close to the river's side.

The braves stood tall and ready for battle.
Their Indian faces were bright with war paint.
This black iron horse with no bridle or saddle,
the white man's dark dragon must be slain.
Groaning up the grade in the blazing sun
she climbed the railed ladder to Pinto Pass.
The shiny iron horse on her maiden run
didn't realze it would be her last.

The tribe made ready for the coming attack.
With ponies and ropes they dragged jagged boulders
around a blind bend where there's no turnin' back.
They laid in wait by the tracks' soiled shoulders.
She crested the tall hill and ran the pass
then she started on her downhill run.
Her eyes were blind to the jagged rock mass
as the steel rails glared in the mid-day sun.

The tracks became a bold funeral pyre
bordered by Indians west and east.
They watched the iron horse explode and expire.
She'd breathe no more this mangled black beast.
This silver-black steed had only one run;
now she's scrap metal strewn under the plain.
She's buried there somewhere in death's dark canyon.
This was her lone run she won't run again.

Marshall Blake's Boy

I remember it like yesterday; the day they deputized him.
Ninety percent of the town turned out to take the happening in.
Jim's boy Matt had grown to be a strapping fine young lad,
and on that day, he'd wear a badge of courage like his dad.

Jim Blake had been the Marshall for nigh on twenty years.
He'd seen the smiles of Cimarron and he'd seen her tears.
The outlaws came and went, and Jim Blake faced them all;
and as men cast their shadows, Jim's was mighty tall.

Jim's boy Matt, the new deputy, wore his badge with pride.
He sauntered into the saloon with an easy manly stride.
He set down at a table at the far end of the bar.
Innocence shone from his face and his new tin star.

Matt ordered whiskey straight, as the doors swung open wide.
There stood an angry stranger; steel hangin' at his side.
He called John Lucas out and growled, "Lucas draw your gun.
Right here's the end of the line for you; there ain't nowhere to run."

Matt stepped in to break it up. He knew John couldn't win.
Someone yelled for the Marshall and as Jim Blake walked in,
The gunfire roared and smoked; then Matt Blake lay there dead.
His first day on the job had bought a bullet in the head.

When the gun smoke finally cleared, Jim knelt down at Matt's side.
A grown man doesn't cry, but a tear fell from his eye.
His son lay in his arms, dead and cold as stone.
Jim had felt alone before, but this was more alone.

I remember it like yesterday, the day they deputized him.
He stood there tall as he received his brand-new badge of tin.
Jim's boy, Matt, was a good boy and everybody's friend.
It was a dirty day in Cimarron, the day Matt's life would end.

Charlie's Dream

They ventured from the east with wishes dreams and hopes,
trekking thru the deserts and cross the mountain slopes;
two weeks out already and five more weeks to go,
heading for the west where the milk and honey flow.
In wagon three was Charlie with his wife and family.
He was going west to find his destiny.
All his life he'd struggled; he was no man of means,
but Charlie was a good man and his dreams were simple dreams.

The wagon train was winding toward the promised land.
Wooden wheels were turning, burning deep tracks in the sand:
Sixty wagons long with just one goal in mind.
Sixty wagons strong to cross the California line.
Charlie's wife Gisele was the kind a poor man needs
to help him build a home and help him plant new seeds.
Charlie's three young sons would help him farm the land
and Charlie's girl Roxanne would take a cowboy's hand.

About the fourth week out the Indians attacked;
bullets from the front and arrows from the back.
The train had formed a circle with wagons overturned,
some hit by flaming arrows, choking as they burned.
The wagon train had stumbled in this strange wild land.
Wooden wheels stopped turning, dug into the sand:
Sixty wagons strong with rifle & gun.
Sixty wagons long with fear in every one.

It took less than an hour until the last man fell.
They killed his wife Gisele in Charlie's private hell.
Roxanne was dragged away in the middle of a scream.
The Indians and arrows murdered Charlie's dream.
The wagon train was cursed and never saw the promised land.
Her wooden wheels stopped turning; no tracks left in the sand:
Sixty wagons long; no trace left where they'd been.
Sixty wagons gone; and lost was Charlie's dream.

Days of the Buffalo

Gone are the days of the buffalo
and Indians hunting with arrow and bow.
Gone is the freedom they once knew before
and sacred hunting grounds sacred no more.

Out on this grassy windswept plain
that feeds on sun and drinks the rain,
once long ago the buffalo roamed
and the Indian had a place to call home.

Alive with the red man's sweat and tears
this plain was nurtured for many years.
It was the old ways of the red man
to take just what he needed from this rich land.

He hunted and fished, and he planted seed
just to survive; not for sport or greed.
The earth was his father, his mother, his son.
The land and the sky and the red man were one.

Then one day the white man rode onto the prairie
and changed the face of the land of the free.
One by one red men went to their graves
as the land of the free made the Indians slaves.

They were here first and this was their land
but they were robbed of it by the white man.
Red blood and white blood spilled on the plain.
The Indians would not own this land again.

We took their land and called it our nation.
We forced them out onto poor reservations.
On sad broken wings the eagle has flown
and the endangered buffalo no longer roam.

Red and White

Each man has his own background, and for the most part too,
each has his own beliefs he carries false or true.
The red man has his ritual ways. The white man has his laws;
and they never fully understand each other's cause.

The white man's had his way in shaping western history.
He's fought hard for the right to say this land of ours is free.
Some live in the big city and dream in their high rise.
Others toil on the land and weep through dusty eyes.

The red man can't be hemmed in or tied to city lights.
He likes the open skies and starry prairie nights.
Fishin' for his breakfast cooked on open flames,
he hunts with a hunger and a thirst that can't be tamed.

The white man has his God and his way of life.
He has his choice of many roads that branch off left and right.
He won't take responsibility for injustices or war
and he won't give the red man back what belonged to him before.

The red man has his great spirit and sacred mother earth.
He knows that wealth and power aren't the measure of one's worth.
He whispers to the rain and listens to the wind
and tries to stay tune with the world he's living in

The red man and the white man roam this earth together.
It's a shame they don't take the time to know each other better.
History's filled with bloodshed and battles left behind
that would not have been fought if man was not so blind.

Each being has a special white magic of his own
and we must take our best part with us thru this vast unknown
As we walk life's crowded pathways, we still walk alone;
and we all reap our destiny from the seed's we've sown.

Rodeo Cowboy

He's headin' down the highway goin' to the rodeo,
dreamin' bout tomorrow the summer sun is sinkin' low.
He's starin' at his saddle rememberin' the times he fell.
Tomorrow night could find him in heaven or in hell.

His mind is drifting' to those dusty white gates.
He's hoping' and prayin' he'll be scorin' straight eights.
He lost everything except his pride and beat up van.
He gave up everything to be a rodeo man.

Take a hard look at his face you can tell he's been around;
sometimes ridin' high sometimes down on the ground.
He loves the rush of the ride and the danger game
ridin' bulls with a suicide knot in the rein.

In his back-hip pocket he packs a tarnished ring;
that long-gone woman was his everything.
The wild side of him just couldn't settle down
and she couldn't take traveling town to town.

That long-gone woman still haunts his weary mind,
but it's too late now to try to walk her line.
He's a road warrior who never sings the blues;
a hard luck hobo who keeps on paying his dues.

The rodeo cowboy is a man who walks alone
on a long hard road that turns a heart to stone.
He's earned all his scars, ridin' the rodeo,
but the deepest wounds are the ones that never show.

Still on the circuit chasin' those dusty rainbows,
that's the life of a cowboy ridin' the rodeos.

Miscellaneous

Rithimus Aeternam

Tumbling Down

Shakespeare said it with quill and ink
and inspiration's golden link
and the words came tumbling down:
in sonnets, verses, plays and prose,
in theatres, and travelling minstrel shows.
His passion still rages and spills from the pages
onto the glitter of sound sets and stages.
Tumbling down ... still tumbling down.

Mozart said it with notes and keys
in compositions and symphonies
and the music came tumbling down:
illuminating the darkness undressing,
devils, angels and lovers confessing
the agonies and ecstasies
in serenades and rhapsodies.
Tumbling down ... still tumbling down.

Michelangelo said it with paints and brush
guided by an angel's touch
and the colours came tumbling down:
onto the Sistine chapel's ceiling,
saints, cherubs, and angels kneeling
in a masterpiece of holiness,
saving grace and forgiveness.
Tumbling down ... still tumbling down.

Artists, Musicians, Poets and Sages
droplets of gold on history's pages
tumbling down throughout the ages.
Their world of beauty surrounds us still.
Their legacy is a living will.
Tumbling down ...
forever tumbling down.

Fading Fingerprint

A modern day painting with Monet splashes
resurrected from yesterday's ashes;
once, a living, breathing, hillside
beneath a translucent, glistening eye
refracting a copper, renaissance sky.
The water ripples and softly whispers
like an old man rubbing his whiskers;
beside an abandoned church in the vale
with cross to the mast and blood on the sail.

I gaze into the future holocaust days.
I see the disasters and the plagues
shaking the four corners of the earth,
spreading destruction and wanton dearth.

And, all the people have disappeared
Inside the moment they most feared;
    the moment of silence
    that followed the violence

And their hearts stopped beating;
nature finally defeating
those who threw caution to the wind;
the non environmentalists as they sinned;
turning the debt riddled wheel of fate;
finally paying a price too great—
Not one human eye left to shed a tear,
Just a faint fading fingerprint we were once here.

Dried Flowers Of Youth

For Rex Howard, July 23, 1930 - November 7, 2012
British Columbia Country Music Hall of Fame inductee 2004

Dried flowers of youth crushed between pages.
Forgotten utterings of ancient sages.
A whisper and scream and the drama between.
Life unravelling at the seam.
A young man running through early chapters,
hobbling toward final ever afters.

You leave this world more every day.
Slowly you're slipping and sliding away
into that nether land of yesterday;
and oh, that I could follow you there
to leave behind this worry and care;
to build with you castles on the beach
in that world you visit when you're out of reach.

Whispers and memories of your sweet song.
When you were young. When you were strong.
Before the years made your bones ache.
Before your hands started to shake.
Before you had to be wheeled in a chair.
Before time left you nothing to spare!

Dried flowers of youth are crumbling now
gracing the stage in their final bow.
Your frailty of heart will soon set you free
and far, far you'll fly away from me
to a place where streets are paved with gold
where dreams cannot be bought or sold;
where music never ceases to play.
It will call to you softly and take you away.

And as you leave this world behind,
the best part of me will become ... undefined.

Parading Through the Ages

Parading through the ages like a fool.
Rebreaking every bloodied broken rule.

A bird with wounded wing in maiden flight
is searching for lost rings of golden light
misplaced when conscience looked the other way
and every good intention went astray.
A pool of pallid water at its feet
as still as if it were an icy sheet.
Sorrow's tears shed from a weary eye
drop from a polished bucket in the sky
where starlight burns and turns its face in shame
with little or no hope of finding fame.

This bird with wounded wing, now flying wild,
is lost and flailing like an unkempt child.
She'll never find her way back to her nest.
She knows not whether it lies east or west.
She rides on lies and travels the fast lane
unaware it holds a world of pain.

Are we not like these birds that flit and fly
with deafened ears that shut out every sigh;
quite unaware of eyes that we make cry
while searching out our big piece of the pie;
not looking back to see the fallout of
the lies we told that broke the hearts we love?

But do we love; or do we lack the depth
to think of someone else with every breath?
And when death forces us at last to kneel
will we be able to change karma's wheel?
Or will we always fly with wounded wing,
trapped in the halo of a broken ring,
parading through the ages like a fool,
rebreaking every bloodied broken rule?

Nostalgia

So many things today have no value anymore.
What happened to the good old days when no one locked their door?

In the old days no one knew the meaning of a home invasion.
When criminals were sent to jail not wrist slapped with probation.
I recall walking to school, not afraid of being kidnapped.
I remember unlocked lockers that never got ransacked.
The days when teachers didn't have to take a student's crap.
The principal stepped in and introduced them to the strap.

I can still remember my Nana's first colour TV;
a strip of three-colour cellophane covering the screen.
Oh, how we loved that three-colour screen; no more black and white.
We stayed up late watching it that memorable first night.

Kids had to make their own fun: kick the can, marbles and tag;
and working at their daily chores was always such a drag.
On allowance day to the corner store all the kids would rush
for jaw breakers, pickaninny gum, marabones and Orange Crush.
Now the days of the corner store are almost gone and done
taken out by the big franchises like "Mac's" and "On The Run".

I used to fuel my car up for less than a five-dollar bill.
Now I almost break the bank with every gasoline fill.
Gone are the days of the street corner pay telephones.
Now we're slaves to Blackberries and Cel phone roaming zones.

Today we've all got computers to keep us occupied.
We walk to the beat with iPod wires dangling at our side.
Things are always changing - nothing ever stays the same.
Our innocence has long been lost and it's a crying shame.

So many things today have no value anymore.
I long for the good old days when no one locked their door.

Coffee Cup Left In The Rain
(A Day In The Life of an Elderly Smoker)

It's a coffee cup left in the rain kind of day,
wishy-washy at best dressed in nondescript gray.
At a table, four perfect strangers sit there.
Coffee cups steaming ghost kites in the air.
Horns blaring as cars rush by on the street.
Pedestrians scrambling with scurrying feet.
A young boy runs by as fast as the breeze.
No white in his hair, no ache in his knees.

At the coffee table's revolving door,
one leaves and another sits down to make four
Seniors on the edge of life watch it pass by
recalling the past with a smile and a sigh.
A guy in the baseball cap's chewing his cud.
On the edge of his collar there's a trace of dried blood.
He has falling down jowls and the eyes of a Raven
and a stubble of whiskers on a face that's unshaven.

A man in a black toque says not a word,
just shakes his head at a world turned absurd.
A lady in blue with a Liverpool cap
wears a heart on her jacket, the left collar flap;
she sits silently blowing ringlets of smoke
wondering how life got to be such a joke.

A guy in a cowboy hat takes off his glove.
He sits in his scooter wrapped in lost love;
memories of yesterday now dead and gone.
In his mind's fireplace the embers live on
and warm him inside on cold days like this
with a soft downy touch and a wet frosty kiss.
He fumbles for his pack of cigarettes;
then for the lighter he sometimes forgets.
He flicks his Bic and his world comes alive.
Without his smokes he couldn't survive.

The baseball cap leaves and a bald head sits down
and pulls out a smoke in coffee table town.
Then a white haired lady in pink bedroom slippers
sits down and pulls out a pair of worn clippers.
There's a bit of small talk but no one says much.
They're out of time, out of sync and out of touch.

An old scruffy man shuffles by very slow,
just putting in time with nowhere to go.
Everything now is a slow motion slide.
He's just one more wave in old age's neap tide.
Time crawls by for these forgotten faces
that wear slip on shoes since they can't tie shoelaces.

Their old ancient bones ache hard and creak.
Their powerless voices are soft when they speak.
Most have got cell phones but none of them ring.
Their friends have all passed ... flown far on the wing.
These seniors once strong now weak and diluted
feel so unrequired in a world convoluted.

At the coffee table's revolving door
one leaves and another sits down to make four.
All perfect strangers, remaining as such,
sometimes there's small talk, but no one says much.
They have one common thread: that white cigarette.
So they band together though they've never met.
In the game of life they've been trumped by the joker
and this is their life as an elderly smoker.

For them, every day is the same as today;
wishy-washy at best dressed in nondescript gray.
But tomorrow they'll congregate back here again
to sip from life's coffee cup left in the rain.

Eulogenic
(aka Higher)

I've walked the summer pathways of love when it's in bloom
and travelled down its alleys of heartaches, tears and gloom.
I've walked through dreams with passion pulling at my sleeve
and learned that love is all that matters. This is my belief.

I've held a baby in my arms and been blessed by its breath.
I've come to trust the Lord and have no fear of death.
I've given up my heart and soul for the sake of love.
I've climbed inside compassion that fit me like a glove.

I've had my share of heartaches but faith has seen me through
the darkest of the starkest nights into a sky of blue.
It's been a destined journey, a long walk to remember
under summer sunsets; through snowstorms in December.

> *And now the days are hazing gray,*
> *shorter every one.*
> *Winter's chill is gaining ground.*
> *The sun is on the run...*

Looking back upon my life I do have some regrets.
I've reaped what I have sewn. I never hedged my bets.
Teardrops falling down my cheeks reflect each smile and frown.
The end of days is drawing near. The sun is going down.

I've tried to run the good race and when I pass away
I hope my words will still live on; in someone's mind they'll stay;
and if perchance they soothe a heart or cause a lover's sigh,
then, higher on an angel's wing this soul of mine shall fly.

Higher on an angel's wing, this soul of mine shall fly.

Winding Road

On life's winding road one can lose one's vision
and pass right by their destiny with the wrong decision.
The key to fame and fortune is knowing where and when.
Knowing where to stand firm; and knowing when to bend.

History's filled with fools; and a few great men and women.
Great ones learn by their mistakes but fools rush in again.
Wise ones live with principles they will not compromise.
Fools keeps chasing rainbows that only cloud their eyes.

What one man calls his medicine; another one calls poison.
Whiskey warms some hearts; drowns others and destroys them.
On this winding road of life we all make our own choices.
We can talk in hazy whispers or speak in strong clear voices.

And what of the road not taken that each of us has seen?
Did it host a nightmare or hold a precious dream?
Once we've passed it by it seems to disappear.
When opportunity knocks, how many of us hear?

We're all a drop of water in this river we call life.
Some live by the written word; and some live by the knife.
Black or yellow, red or white, Christians, Muslims, Jews,
Each one has their cross to bear and each must pay their dues.

When we come into this life we know not what it holds.
Some hearts have a rusty seam; some are sown with gold.
But one thing is for certain in life's haphazard game,
we come into this world alone and leave it just the same.

A Sigh Or A Shout

The best part's not knowing how it all turns out.
Does it end with a sigh or end with a shout?
The wondering grows stronger every single year.
Does it end with a whimper and a hard-edged tear?
Or, does it just keep on giving and bending
on a journey and trek that is never-ending?
Do we simply end to begin once again
as kindred spirits wrapped in love and pain?
Returning once again back to each other
in new disguises, and undercover?
And does karmic tension dance on a thread
as we climb back into each other's bed?

Once upon a time it seemed so simple
like a child's smile and laughing dimple;
innocent whispers nudging our hearts
oblivious to the fate life imparts.
We continue to sojourn, sometimes world weary,
down pathways and trails uncertain and dreary,
hoping to find that lost link of gold;
searching for dreams to have and to hold
close to our chest to warm us at night,
cleansing our wrongs and wringing them right.

And then one day, on a cold hard rock,
we hear the rattle and hum of death's knock;
and run as we may, we can't run away.
The hour is here and it's judgement day,
so we fall to our knees in a show of trust
beseeching the powers and begging they must
forgive us our sins as we didn't know
the depth of the scar when we struck the blow.
Will it be loud or soft when the end comes?
A raging heartbeat or an echo of drums?
The best part is not knowing how it turns out;
if it ends with a sigh or ends with a shout.

Quaint and Shoddy

On the dank west corner, where vine and gate mingle,
there's a quaint shoddy house of cement and wrinkle.
She shudders and breathes in a crypt of nightmares.
Sometimes I hear whispers from under the stairs,
chanting and casting spells to slow her aging;
to outrun death's storm and its savage raging.

On the eastern edge of hedges and flowers
this unkempt abode has clocked too many hours
and years of inequity, love, loss and hate;
undigested, bitter, sour to the taste.
A bankrupt waste of fury and emotion;
this landlocked ship down on a dry rot ocean.

On the northern reflection of heartache and tears
hazy ghosts and sad clowns parade through the years.
I peer through a cracked mirror and see myself
elderly and ravaged on time's rusty shelf.
A southern sun's glare opens my eyes up wide.
There's nowhere to run to and no place to hide.

Like that quaint, shoddy house, how frail I've become.
I rue dreams I left undone and songs unsung.
Behind the tall walls and barbed wire of my mind
regrets and resentments begin to unwind.
Scratchy film clips flash in front of my eyes.
The truth rips its mask off and sheds its disguise.

It's been a short journey but in the long run
I see what I was and what I've become.
Restless ghosts riding the winds of yesterday
are chasing me down; I can't chase them away.
And fate has me squared in the sights of her gun.
The end's closing in on my fast setting sun.

I stand quaint and shoddy at eternity's door
awaiting final judgement on heaven's shore.

Tag You're It!

"Tag. You're it!"

I hear those words echoing still.
Yesterday's sounds in a high pitched trill.
Laughter ringing from days of old.
The stain of rain still damp on the soul.
Knee deep in memory's steep castle keep
when laughter was easy to come by like sleep;
Before the shadow of gray days crept in
on the little cat feet of some other sin.

Born of a wish tangled in a cross,
precious moments were lost or tossed
to winds of change fading from sight.
Wasting our days and chasing the night
the sun rose at noon, and always too soon.
Chasing the daylight into the moon,
dreams we were chasing fell by the way
and now we're miles past yesterday.

Born in the sunshine, the snow and the rain,
when we think it's over, it begins again.
Parading through faces, and changing names,
we keep running around in circle games.
It matters not our position or fame,
we're all born to be cast to soil or flame.
Trading places with death on life's page
we spiral in circles back to its stage.

As the wheel of destiny spins its choice,
an impish elf states in a loud raspy voice…

"Tag. You're it!"

City of Dreams

(Tribute to the City of New Westminster, BC CANADA)

A pale, purple twilight splashed with sky feathers,
Drifts in wisps and loosened tethers.
A surreal tapestry hangs above.
Chandeliers of stars are sprinkling love,
embracing the last remnants of sunlight
peeking through the scattered moonlight ...
This is New Westminster tonight!

White specks glow in the amber shine;
sparkling diamonds on the evening skyline.
The jewelled fingers of night prance and romance,
Reflecting and pooling, they shadow dance
with the shimmering Fraser River starlight ...
This is the City of Dreams tonight!

Inherent mood music's written and pinned
on this sultry, warm summer evening wind.
Unravelling, unspooling their magical weave,
dreams spill from an angel's sleeve
in the hush of a wish and a sacred bow
and the residue of a sacrosanct vow.
Reminiscent of a smooth satin feeling,
they're laced with enchantment that sets the heart reeling,
in the ambient glow of soft candlelight ...
This is New Westminster tonight!

A touch of glory, magic in the air;
A drifting of memories everywhere;
A footprint on life's water; a ripple on the earth;
A whisper on the wind; a diamond of great worth;
Indestructible!

Dressed in a necklace of pearl moonlight
this is New Westminster tonight.

This is the City of Dreams!

Wounded Stone Angel

She's a wounded stone angel, a bittersweet vine
mired in dark dreams, scarred with stale wine.
She's a midnight dancer carved in cement;
a clumsy participant inside a lament.

Chained to a path of hidden dangers
and written into a book of strangers
she masquerades through pages and chapters
searching for lost happy ever-afters.

She's insoluble water in a prison of fire,
a wounded breath exhaled with desire
trapped in the dark of an oil slicked river,
shaking inside a hot fevered shiver.

She doesn't go near mirrors. She wears a disguise.
She doesn't want to see her slit paper cut eyes;
or the jagged incision of her butchered smile
that she hasn't seen in such a long while.
So she peers through the streaked windows of her heart
to find a new landscape and make a new start.

She's a wounded stone angel bound at the wrists
dancing to old rusty records and discs.

Condemned like a prisoner on the green mile,
she compacts herself into a lopsided smile
and slowly dissolves into dust on the wind
leaving no remnant that's she's ever been.

She's a wounded stone angel travelling light and alone
leaving no traces or scars on the stone.

A Tricky Thing

The past is a tricky thing.

Ghostly images haze through the twilight zone.
Some are wrapped in water; some are etched in stone.
Viewed through filmy glasses they glow in soft stardust
before the hard-edged glare of truth exposes hidden rust.

The road is long and winding from past to present day.
Unscheduled stops can crop up as we go our way:
Some a sparkling breath of effervescent air;
Some the stifling remnants of a stale nightmare.

In the stone cold sober aftermath of the tricky past
or at the murky bottom of a filmy half-full glass,
the past sneaks up on us dressed in a thin disguise;
and when we least expect it, it smacks us in the eyes.

At the quantum level, gazing through a filmy glass,
the present is obsessed with its own distorted past.
It stares in awe and wonders how it ever got this way.
Revolving and evolving, from black and white to gray
it's always there to haunt us; it never fades away.

The past is … a tricky thing.

Crazy World

Taking a mind trip past the horizon
I suddenly find I'm dimensionalizing
into a harbour of surreal moonbeams.
I'm travelling down a river of dreams,
Riding the groove of a split decision,
Escaping from my crumbling prison.

I see bubble gum, sealing wax, butterfly wings
and a puppet dangling on threadbare strings
dancing to a cracked digeridoo
and an off-key singer who hasn't a clue.

Then I see the Red Sea splitting apart.
A Pharaoh and soldiers served up a la carte.
I quickly grab onto a punctured life jacket
and then it turns into a white tennis racquet.

Sponge Bob and Squidward have skipped out of school
And Batman and Robin are playing it cool.
The Rivers of Babylon flow in between.
It all seems so real, but I know it's a dream.

Slipping and sliding into the night
remains of the day slowly fade from sight.
I sew myself into a blanket of dreams.
I rest in the palm of sleep's satin seams
as I leave this crazy world behind
in the prismed recesses of my mind.

Through the Broken Looking Glass

Alone on my patio late at night
under the breast of pearl moonlight
travails of the day begin to fade
and sometimes great decisions are made.
I pull on the shaft of a cigarette
dwelling on deeds I've lived to regret.
Smoke rises, forms rings and starts to flow.
Memories take form in the afterglow.
Ten floors up, too low and too high
to properly measure the depth of a sigh;
but sigh I do and live with rue
for the many things I didn't do.

I didn't spend enough time with the trees
or listening to the voice of the breeze.
My family should have been first on my mind
but work and play let them fall behind.
In every role I played a part
I wish I'd worn a kinder heart.
So many things I didn't do;
the time I didn't spend with you
and now it's too late to atone
for past emotions never shown.

The dimming of the light appears.
I feel the burning sting of tears
threatening to fall from my eyes
and shatter my well worn disguise.
At last you'll see how much I cared
although these feelings were unshared.
So powerful the pull of death.
So bittersweet this final breath.
Forgive me for things I didn't do
and know I was always loving you.
I finally leave you here alone;
my body turned to cold, cold stone.

The Empty Women

With all they love stripped from them,
they are ... the empty women.

They peer through the ageless passing of years.
They stare though icicles heavy with tears.
With wounded hearts, on bended knees,
they claw at locked doors that have no keys.
Submerged in the waters of eternity,
they wring their hands in futility.
These empty women stare through the deep
at the rough path ahead and a mountain too steep.
Clad in old slippers tattered and worn
they stand in the avalanche of a storm.
They walk as old ghosts from cold graves risen
searching for exit doors out of this prison.
With numb, bleeding feet they walk, then they crawl,
trapped with no hope of scaling hell's wall.
These empty women keep paying the cost
for shell-shocked dreams and yesterdays lost.

A hard rain falls like a poisonous potion
creating a vague jigsaw-puzzled ocean,
crashing a beach strewn with broken seashells,
harbouring dark secrets it never tells.
Accentuating the absence of love,
stars fall from a black velour mantle above;
embers aglow in the ashtray of night
caught in the jaws of lust's fatal bite.

Invisible now, erased by dawn's wet glove,
they're forgotten women abandoned by love.
They're the elegy of a dark broken moon,
lost in a midnight eclipse at high noon.
Their freedom and hope were lost in the blink
of death's sordid eyelid feigning a wink,
blotting out their oceans of tears
and the empty days of all their years.

Their footprints will dissolve and leave no mark;
no trace of their hungry cries in the dark;
no mention of their deep desperation.
This is their history … the world's aberration.

Empty women, past the point of return,
these butterflies born, only to burn,
twisting inside the cocoon of death's kiss.
in this moment that's lost, but still always is.

Invisible trapped in a nightmarish dream,
these women are the primal scream.

With all they love stripped from them,

      they are …
         the empty women.

Shadow Shapes

Peaceful creatures on our Earthen shore,
The Woolly Mammoths walk here no more.

Holding court on ever dwindling grasslands
Did their extinction come from human hands?
Or from cataclysmic meteor strikes?
Or when icebergs broke through nature's dyke?
Or did the quick onset of climate change
drive them further afield to roam a new range?
They kept on moving just to escape
dead vegetation and a barren landscape.

They retreated thousands of years ago
to Russia's pasturelands scattered with snow;
then emerging trees waged war on their land
took over the plains where they made their last stand.

Commonplace, once, on Eurasia's face;
years ago vanished without a trace;
furry and large tusked herbivores;
colossal, huge, giant hulks of yore.

Peaceful creatures on our Earthen shore,
the Woolly Mammoths walk here no more.

Aftermath

Time's the great healer of wounds and slaughters
that scar broken hearted sons and daughters.

These days when your image crosses my mind
it lingers not... flashes past and I find
my longing for you has been buried somewhere
and it seems unreal how much I used to care.

For awhile I could recall only good times.
Now looking back, I remember love crimes.
The verbal abuse and not giving a damn
led me to the slaughter like a trusting lamb.
Sure you were there through the good and the thin,
but through thick and bad times you were out, you weren't in.

I wonder, now, who I was when I loved you,
a narcissistic liar who couldn't be true.
I must have misplaced my own self esteem
somewhere inside your nightmarish dream.

You left me without a thought and walked away
leaving me locked inside love's tragic play.
I cried a river ... no, it was an ocean.
I thought I'd die from this strangled emotion.
Heartache held hands with me each waking hour
and battled with sleep in night's tear filled tower
but time the great healer threw off my sorrow
and fulfilled her promise of a brand-new tomorrow.

I thank God above and the universe
for taking this bitter cup, lifting this curse.

Now, if ever you cross my mind, you disappear.
I have nothing left for you, not even a tear.

The Promise

After the bloodshed and the tears,
after the war of the final years;
the eyes of the blind shall see again,
and every heart shall be free again.

The children of God will gather round.
The lost little sheep shall all be found.
God will wipe away every tear.
Pain and heartache will disappear.

The lame will walk without a cane.
The lion will lay with the lamb again.
The old will be young and have no fear;
and the deaf will hear God's word so clear.

No more hunger and no more strife.
This is the promise ... Eternal Life.
When God smiles down on me and you
the promise of paradise will come true.

Remember the promise Jesus made
that holy day in the mountain glade:
A white horse will soar down from the sky;
Faithful & True the Lord will abide.

God's light will shine brighter than the sun.
He'll smile down on his chosen ones.
When He smiles down on me and you
The promise of paradise will come true.

When God smiles down on me and you
The promise of paradise will come true.

Keepers of the Birthright

We are the sanctuary of life.
We are the keepers of the birthright.

We are the women of the world.
We give life with our hearts unfurled.
Blessed with the sacrament of the womb,
we are your breath from cradle to tomb.

We are the keepers of the birthright.
Mothers and daughters, star-seed and sunlight.
We are the sustenance and the love.
We are the keepers, below and above.

We are the blood flowing through your veins.
We give you shelter from life's hurricanes.
We are the flesh sustaining your soul.
We give you warmth that conquers all cold.

Give us alms for the breath we give and impart;
and salve for the wounds we bear in our heart.

We are the sanctuary of life.
We are the keepers of the birthright.

Martyr

On a precipice of cliff sky-high and steep,
there overlooking eternity deep,
I saw his fleeting ghost arise
trailing stardust and tears 'cross the skies.

On the left the angels were singing songs.
On the right the demons hovered in throngs.
Who would lay claim to his soul in their game?
Would he be taken in glory or shame?

Some things we know not the measure of;
some spirits fall, some soar with the dove.
Was he an angel in devil's disguise?
Or was he the devil as most did surmise?

He was who he was in battle and reverence.
For better of worse this man made a difference.
When cornered a lion will fight to its death.
What were his thoughts as he took his last breath?

Is he lost to the night or reborn to the light?
Martyr or villain, what will history write?

The Final Collapse

I am a house of cards:
Words, music and dreams
collapsing and resurrecting
in new colour schemes.

People enter my world unafraid
to spin my well-worn wheel retrograde,
where Kings and Jokers vie for aces
and Jacks and Queens wear poker faces.

I'm balancing on the edge of a plate,
dining with destiny, supping with fate.
I collapse and arise like a weary phoenix
brushing off sparks from the fiery mix.

I'm an aging house of well-used cards
grasping for lost words, music and dreams,
moving into the final collapse
and coming apart at the ragged seams.

Death's bony finger is wagging and beckoning
calling me to my final reckoning.
I'm searching for clues or discarded road maps
as I head toward my final collapse.

Happy New Year

Tonight I'm recalling
good times and old friends
as a new chapter starts
and an old one ends.

Time moves on;
this is now; that was then;
and the days of old gold
won't come again.

So raise a glass
to memories gone by
and pay homage to
the tear in your eye.

As one-year fades
into history
a new one arrives
filled with mystery.

Best wishes for
a great new year run
and remember the best
is yet to come.

Judgement Day

I've kicked over the traces
of people and places
that didn't quite fit my dreams.
I tossed them away
like clothes torn and frayed
and coming apart at the seams.

I've walked lonely street
in rain, snow and sleet
and threw caution to the wind;
spoke many a word
better left unheard;
words I can never rescind.

And now at the end
I break. I don't bend
as I reap the crop of my seeds.
It's judgement day
and now I must pay
for all my sordid misdeeds.

May light shine on this heart of coal
and God have mercy on my soul.

Lost Angel

By a highway south of Vegas there's an eagle standing guard;
silver wings and blazing eyes shining cold and hard.
He's seen heroes and angels fencing grace and death.
Did he see you on the run with no place to rest?

There must be a million phone lines from Vegas running south
tracing every secret 'til all the words fade out;
miles and miles of hungry static chewing through the wire
chasing lost angels with wings of burning fire.

Did the eagle finally call to you? Did the endless roads combine
into one long winding highway, one white solid line?
You've flown too far past Eden, lost what you left behind.
Now you're just a lonely shadow fading on life's blind.

Lost angel you've crossed the line. This time you've flown too far
where no one else can find you or hear your beating heart.
A storm's gathering teardrops. The sky is raining pain.
You're on the lonely side of heaven and can't come home again.

You're on the lonely side of heaven
and can't come home again.

A Hieroglyph of Thought

A sonnet is a hieroglyph of thought
with meanings buried deep inside the ink.
At times it wanes to cool then waxes hot
to coax a tear, to cause an eye to blink.
A ghostly image hazing in and out.
A house of mirrors, fiction bending truth.
A whisper hiding in a blatant shout.
A bitter vetch stirred in a sweet vermouth
The written words spilled on the page have dried;
but still they resonate within the mind.
The heartaches, longing, passion, lust and pride
are set in metric form and thus refined.

The remnants of a poetic refrain:
Words echoing in shadows of the rain.

This Realm

There are so many roads that call to us
and lying prophets that covet our trust;
so many pitfalls that can bring us down.
Will we be seen as a sage or clown?

Our days are numbered right from the start.
We have to choose if our head rules our heart.
We have to ponder then we must decide
if we will walk or if we'll ride.

The easy path is not always the best.
The harder may prove the better test
to show the fabric of your inner soul;
to see how you rock and the way you roll.

But one thing's for sure my kindred friend;
each start and beginning has its own end.
We chart our journey and choose our path
and learn our truth in the aftermath.

From whence we're born 'til impending death
we walk through dreams of crystal meth.
We are the dreamers and we are the dreams;
and nothing in this realm is what it seems.

Leading Me

And there I was alone stumbling through the dark,
spinning strange illusions in a make-believe park,
walking down a quarter-line, spinning on a dime,
stepping in and out of the mirrors of time,
measuring my tiny steps, trying not to fall
as if there still were time, and yet no time at all.

The clock of heaven sighed and rubbed her hands together
then struck the midnight hour with her palm of leather.
I raised my eyes to heaven, gave thanks and took a bow.
I knew what truly mattered would manifest right now...
And there you were approaching me inside illusion's park,
reaching for my trembling hand to lead me past the dark,
to take me far beyond this corner of the night
into your blazing circle of never-ending light.

Now after all this time... when all seems lost but time,
I've crossed that shaky quarter-line and I've spent my last dime
Finally escaping the mirrors of time,
I take a long hard look at what I've left behind.
I see the mirrors cracking and the clock of heaven fall.

And now there is no time ...
No time left at all.

Alberta Street

On the brow of the hill on Alberta Street
I gaze at the dove-tailed narrowing view
where the river and buildings silently meet
and Port Mann Bridge accents the blue.

I hear the guttural growl of a mower
against the high pitched keen of a gull.
As time and tide move closer and slower
the waves from the tugboats shine the dull.

Somewhere a homeless man wheels a cart
through the back alleys of the filthy rich,
watching his back and always on guard.
One false step and he's in the ditch.

Up in the trees the oblivious birds
pay no attention to the vagrant below
and Miss Muffet is eating her whey and curds
as the eyes of the spider spin and glow.

The wise man remembers. The fool forgets
there's always some bitter mixed with the sweet.
The morning sun rises; the evening sun sets
on the brow of the hill on Alberta Street.

Hollow Man Burning

The hard edged rumor of impending death
foreshadowing the tragedy at hand.
The promises forsworn with bated breath.
Unanswered prayers reign over shadowland.
A paper king trades places with a clown;
an alcoholic drunkard on the town;
A barstool for a throne, smoke for a crown,
and every drink he takes just takes him down.
He can't escape. He has nowhere to go,
encapsulated in a web of dread.
A mad fool ruling kingdoms rapt with woe,
imprisoned in this nightmare of the dead.

Addicted and enslaved by his desire,
a hollow man burns out in liquor's fire.

Dream

All my days have been a dream
unravelling at its tattered seam,
spilling inglorious indecisions
onto vague nights and indistinct visions:
Chasing the moon past the edge of the sun.
Watching the spectre of stars come undone.
Reshaping a whisper into a scream.
All my days have been a dream.

I'm but a shadow in a dream
professing that which least I seem.
I stand amid the fog and gloom
beneath a raging sky of doom.
I hold within my aching palm
the residue of sorrow's calm
where doubt and hope criss-cross and creep
in seas of heartache hot and deep.
My eyes are burnt I cannot weep.
I'm half awake but still asleep.

The echo of a midnight gasp
fades in words I cannot grasp.
I watch the light of day elapse.
I see the dream I am collapse.

I stand unravelling at the seam
inside this dream within a dream.

All my days have been a dream;
just a dream … just a dream.

Whimsy

The Long and the Short of It

I ordered some cosmic soup and ate my share of crow.
I thought I had arrived but still had far to go.
I met a seagull wading and strolling on the shore.
We spoke of many things and thought we'd both been here before.

We spoke of time and space and the universe divide.
We waded deeper in and spoke of time and tide.
He told me of his time in Spain and the insurrection.
I said I was with Jesus at his resurrection.

We bantered back and forth with some truth but mostly lies.
He was a regal seagull; that much I could surmise.
We talked of composition, poetry and prose
and some obscure writers no-one recalls or knows.

He said he'd been a courier before he broke his wing.
I told him I'd played football but only second string.
We'd both dabbled in painting but never learned to draw.
He said his crow wife left him because he couldn't caw.

Some pelicans were fishing at the water's edge.
An eagle perched and preened on a rocky ledge.
The seagull turned to me and said by the way my name is Dick.
I said my name's Cornelius but my friends just call me Slick.

Engrossed in conversation the time had slipped away.
The clouds were rolling in and covering up the day
I bent down to shake his wing just before we split
and that's my tall tale story … well, the long and short of it.

Chauffeur Driven Dream

Off on another chauffeur driven dream
I'm taking a ride in my ritzy limousine

My imagination is at it again.
No use to fight, I'll give it free rein.
I'll take a trip to the outer reaches
where there's only surf and sunlit beaches.

Inside this chauffeur driven dream,
relaxed inside my warm moonbeam,
sipping cognac and sparkling champagne,
I reduce my mind to a Rorschach ink stain.

I see many patterns dancing in tandem;
blots and circles spreading at random.
A piece of my mind sits on the left side
near a merry-go-round I'm dying to ride.

After a while I tire of this game.
The whole idea seems very lame.
Weary of gathering dust on the shelf
I start to come back into myself.

I cast off my disguise of evil oppressor
and return to my role as an English professor.
The champagne and cognac are fading away
dissolving the dream in the wake of their sway.

My imagination has now crashed and burned
but the lesson still hasn't been learned...
I'm heading back to my chauffeur driven dream
for another wild ride in my fake limousine.

Cirque Déjà-Vu

In a dream I saw iron maidens dancing with dragons
and chimpanzees racing in souped-up, red wagons.
An acrobat flew high on a flying trapeze
and danced on a tightrope with eloquent ease.

In a cirque déjà-vu happening in my dream
the real and unreal are not what they seem.
Elephants are juggled by ballerinas at rest
and gorillas are housed in a small treetop nest.

Lions and tiger are tamed by wild mice
and clowns have turned ugly and aren't very nice.
The bearded lady's lost all the hair on her face.
There's not one strand left; not even a trace.

The fat lady's training to walk the high wire
and the fire-eating man's been proved a big liar.
Trained dogs in costumes are really not trained at all
chasing their tails disobeying every call.

The weary iron maidens have stopped dancing with dragons
and the chimpanzees have parked all their red wagons.
My dream has dissolved melting into the dawn
and the cirque déjà vu is now faded and gone.

Dreaming of Freedom
(Ekphrastic poem written to painting of same name by Hanna Barbara Berwid)

Spinning around in a circle-drome world,
in dreams unfettered, they're coming unfurled.
Tired of their stationary place on the wheel,
they've unwrapped the present and broken the seal.

They've stood at a standstill for many a day:
June through November; December through May.
In the fantasy world of the merry-go-round
their slipping their halters, coming unbound.

As they leap from the floor of the carousel
they're filled with the stories they've heard children tell
about that old Big Rock Candy Mountain
and Willy Wonka's Chocolate Fountain.

They fly through the air with the greatest of ease
chasing the moment, they're ready to seize.
Dreaming of freedom they've mounted time's stage,
leaving the past behind, coming of age.

Candice James Profile:

Candice James served 2 terms (2010-2016) as Poet Laureate of New Westminster BC CANADA and was appointed Poet Laureate Emerita by the City of New Westminster in November, 2016. She is a visual artist; a musician; a singer/songwriter; a workshop facilitator , book reviewer; and the author of fifteen books of poetry. Her poetry has appeared in a variety of international anthologies and magazines.

Candice's artwork has appeared in many magazines internationally including Duende (Goddard University of Fine Arts, Vermont); SurVision, (Ireland); The Arts and Entertainment Magazine (Hollywood); CQ International, (New York); and Wax, Poetry Art Magazine (Canada)

She is also Founder of Royal City Literary Arts Society; Poetic Justice; Poetry in the Park; Poetry New Westminster; RCLAS Singer Songwriters; Fred Cogswell Award for Excellence in Poetry and she is the recipient of the Bernie Legge Artist Cultural Award and Pandora's Collective Citizenship Award.

For further info visit *https://en.wikipedia.org/wiki/Candice_James* *www.silverbowpublishing.com* or *www.candicejames.com*